300+ MAGNETS
IN PLASTIC CANVAS

If you're "attracted" to magnets, 300+ Magnets in Plastic Canvas *is guaranteed to keep you mesmerized! This irresistible new collection of Leisure Arts' best designs includes a variety of quick-and-easy projects that are simple for beginners and fun for veteran stitchers, too. You'll find a multitude of magnetic themes — from seasonal and holiday projects to teddy bears and garden motifs. Your favorite hobbies and animals are also represented, as well as magnets with a touch of country charm. This book is definitely a "must have" for your plastic canvas library!*

LEISURE ARTS, INC.
Little Rock, Arkansas

300+ MAGNETS
IN PLASTIC CANVAS

EDITORIAL STAFF

Vice President and Editor-in-Chief:
Anne Van Wagner Childs
Executive Director: Sandra Graham Case
Editorial Director: Susan Frantz Wiles
Publications Director: Carla Bentley
Creative Art Director: Gloria Bearden
Senior Graphics Art Director: Melinda Stout

PRODUCTION
Managing Editor: Mary Sullivan Hutcheson
Senior Project Coordinator:
Merrilee Gaither Gasaway
Project Coordinators: Catherine Hubmann
and Sherry James
Project Assistants: Lylln Craig and Janie Wright

EDITORIAL
Managing Editor: Linda L. Trimble
Coordinating Editor: Terri Leming Davidson
Associate Editor: Darla Burdette Kelsay
Editorial Associates: Stacey Robertson Marshall
and Janice Teipen Wojcik

DESIGN
Design Director: Patricia Wallenfang Sowers

ART
Crafts Art Director: Rhonda Hodge Shelby
Senior Production Artist: Brent Miller
Production Artists: Keith Melton, Chris Meux,
Katie Murphy, Dana Vaughn, Mary Ellen Wilhelm,
and Karen L. Wilson
Photography Stylists: Beth Carter, Laura Reed,
and Courtney Jones

PROMOTIONS
Managing Editor: Marjorie Ann Lacy
Associate Editors: Dixie L. Morris, Jennifer Ertl
Wobser, and Ellen J. Clifton
Publishing Systems Administrator: Cindy Lumpkin
Publishing Systems Assistants: Susan Mary Gray and
Robert Walker

BUSINESS STAFF

Publisher: Bruce Akin
Vice President and General Manager:
Thomas L. Carlisle
Retail Sales Director: Richard Tignor
Vice President, Retail Marketing: Pam Stebbins

Retail Marketing Director: Margaret Sweetin
Retail Customer Service Manager: Carolyn Pruss
General Merchandise Manager: Cathy Laird
Vice President, Finance: Tom Siebenmorgen
Distribution Director: Rob Thieme

Library of Congress Catalog Number 98-65611
International Standard Book Number 1-57486-096-8

TABLE OF CONTENTS

Happy Hold-ups

*Inspired by the carefree joys of summertime,
our cheery magnets will brighten your
day — any time of the year!*

Flower and
Garden Show
10:00 Sa...

APPY HOLD-UPS

pprox. size: 2³/₄"w x 2³/₄"h each

upplies: Worsted weight yarn or Needloft® astic Canvas Yarn and DMC embroidery oss (refer to color key), one 0¹/₂" x 13¹/₂" sheet of 7 mesh plastic anvas, #16 tapestry needle, magnetic rip, and craft glue.

titches used: Backstitch, Cross Stitch, ench Knot, Fringe Stitch, Gobelin Stitch, osaic Stitch, Overcast Stitch, Scotch Stitch, eversed Tent Stitch, and Tent Stitch.

Instructions: Follow chart to cut and stitch desired magnet, working backstitches and fringe stitch last. Referring to photo for yarn color, cover unworked edges. Glue magnetic strip to back of magnet.

For Balloon string: Cut a 5" length of red yarn. Referring to photo, thread yarn length through Balloon at ★. Secure end of yarn length on back of Balloon.

For Kite tail: Cut a 5" length of orange yarn. Referring to photo, secure one end of yarn length on back of Kite. Cut a 4" length each of blue, green, and red yarn. Tie each yarn length into a knot around Kite tail; trim ends.

Designs by Ann Townsend.

Kite (18 x 24 threads)

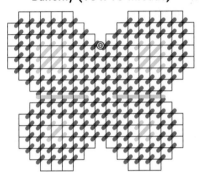

COLOR (NL)	
▨	white (41)
▨	yellow (57)
▨	gold (11)
▨	orange (52)
▨	pink (55)
▨	red (01)
▨	blue (35)
▨	dk blue (32)
▨	green (28)
▨	brown (13)
⊙	yellow (57) Fr. knot
◎	brown (13) fringe

COLOR (DMC)	
▨	*black (310)

*Use 6 strands of floss.

Flower (18 x 18 threads)

Butterfly (18 x 15 threads)

Balloon (16 x 19 threads)

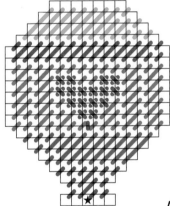

Tulip Pot (18 x 21 threads)

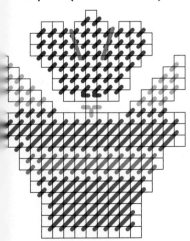

Sun (22 x 14 threads)

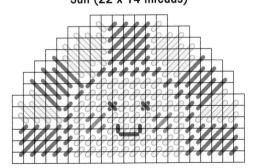

Apple Basket (16 x 16 threads)

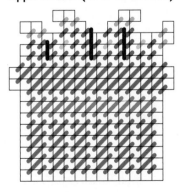

International Flags

Take a trip around the world with these colorful flag magnets! They'll add international flair to your message center, refrigerator, or anywhere else you choose to display them.

INTERNATIONAL FLAGS

Size: 2"w x 1¹/₂"h each

Supplies: Sport weight yarn (refer to color key), one 10¹/₂" x 13¹/₂" sheet of 10 mesh plastic canvas, #20 tapestry needle, magnetic strip, and craft glue.

Stitches used: Backstitch, Cross Stitch, Overcast Stitch, and Tent Stitch.

Instructions: Follow chart to cut and stitch desired magnet, working backstitches last. Using gold overcast stitches, cover unworked edges. Glue magnetic strip to back of magnet.

Designs by Diane W. Villano

COLOR	
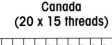 white	
	yellow
	red
	lt blue
	blue
	green
	rust
	black
	*white
	*red
	gold - use for overcast only
*Use 2 plies of yarn.	

Canada
(20 x 15 threads)

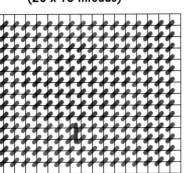

Scotland
(20 x 15 threads)

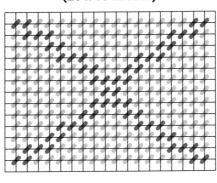

Italy
(20 x 15 threads)

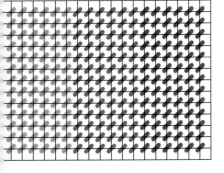

France
(20 x 15 threads)

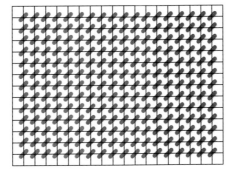

Ireland
(20 x 15 threads)

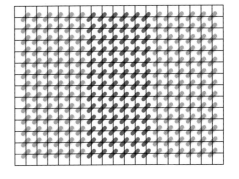

United States
(21 x 15 threads)

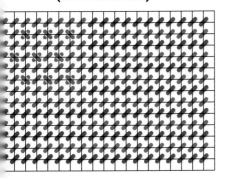

Great Britain
(21 x 15 threads)

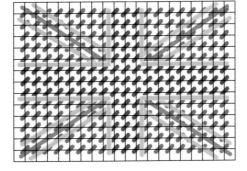

Germany
(21 x 15 threads)

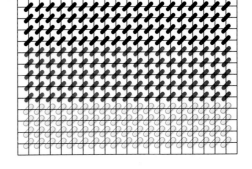

Summer Seashells

Evoke memories of a summer day at the beach with these handsome shell magnets. The stunning seaside treasures are great for showing off vacation photos, artwork, and more.

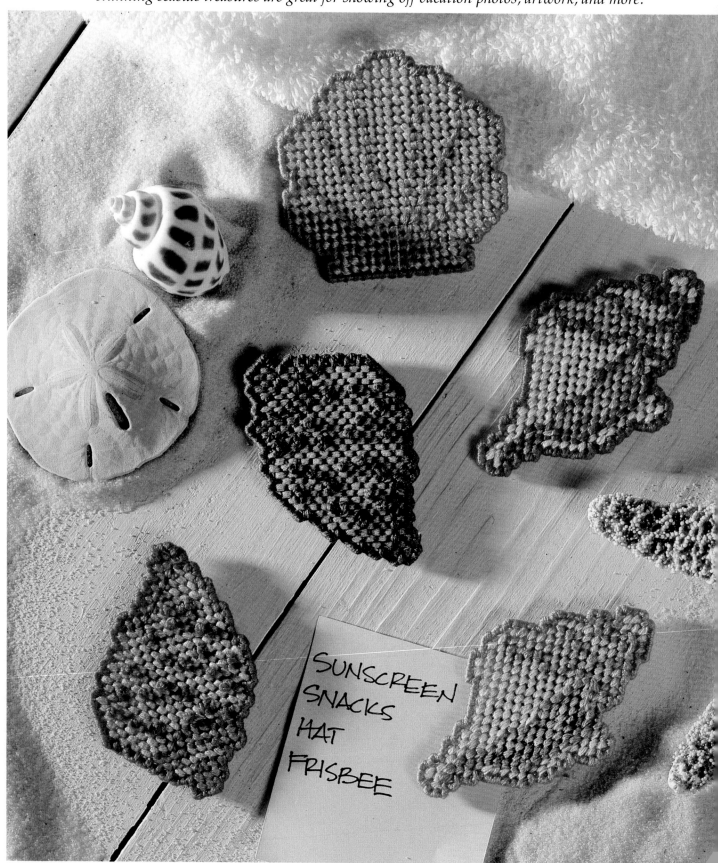

UMMER SEASHELLS

pprox. size: 2¹/₂"w x 2¹/₄"h each

upplies: DMC embroidery floss (refer to color keys), one 10¹/₂" x 13¹/₂" sheet of 0 mesh plastic canvas, #20 tapestry edle, magnetic strip, and craft glue.

itches used: Backstitch, Cross Stitch, ench Knot, Overcast Stitch, Reversed Tent tch, and Tent Stitch.

structions: Use 12 strands of embroidery ss for all stitching. Alternate color keys e given for Shell #2 and Shell #3. Follow art to cut and stitch desired magnet in sired color scheme, working backstitches d French knots last. Glue magnetic strip back of magnet.

esigns by Eleanor Albano.

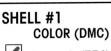

SHELL #1
COLOR (DMC)

✎	lt peach (754) - 5 yds
✎	peach (353) - 7 yds
✎	dk peach (352) - 7 yds

Shell #1 (25 x 25 threads)

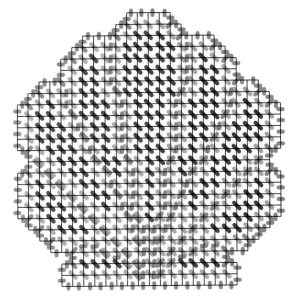

PINK SHELL #2
COLOR (DMC)

✎	lt pink (761) - 6 yds
✎	pink (760) - 1 yd
✎	dk pink (3328) - 6 yds
●	dk pink (3328) Fr. knot

TAUPE SHELL #2
COLOR (DMC)

✎	lt taupe (644) - 6 yds
✎	taupe (642) - 1 yd
✎	dk taupe (3790) - 6 yds
●	dk taupe (3790) Fr. knot

Shell #2 (28 x 19 threads)

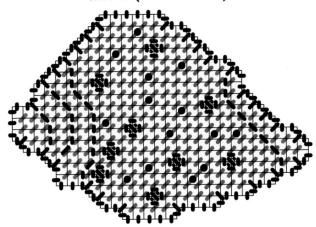

PINK SHELL #3
COLOR (DMC)

✎	lt pink (761) - 2 yds
✎	lt pink (761)
✎	pink (760) - 1 yd
✎	pink (760)
✎	dk pink (3328) - 5 yds
✎	beige (543) - 5 yds

PEACH SHELL #3
COLOR (DMC)

✎	lt peach (754) - 1 yd
✎	peach (353) - 1 yd
✎	dk peach (352) - 5 yds
✎	beige (543) - 5 yds
✎	lt taupe (644) - 1 yd
✎	taupe (642) - 1 yd

Shell #3 (23 x 25 threads)

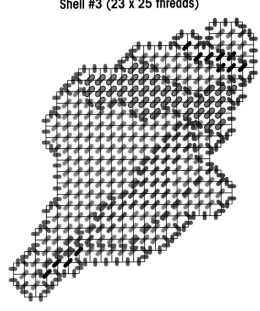

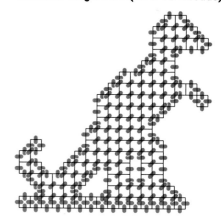

Dinosaur Magnet #1 (18 x 18 threads)

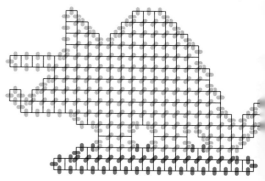

Dinosaur Magnet #2 (24 x 15 threads)

Dandy Dinosaurs

For tons of fun, let your kids create these "dino-mite" magnets! The prehistoric set is sure to capture their imaginations.

DINOSAURS

Approx. size: 2³/₄"w x 2¹/₄"h each
Supplies: Worsted weight yarn (refer to color key), one 10¹/₂" x 13¹/₂" sheet of 7 mesh plastic canvas, #16 tapestry needle, magnetic strip, and craft glue.
Stitches used: Backstitch, Overcast Stitch, and Tent Stitch.
Instructions: Follow chart to cut and stitch desired magnet. Glue magnetic strip to back of magnet.

Designs by Dick Martin.

COLOR	
▨	yellow
▨	orange
▨	blue
▨	green

Dinosaur Magnet #3 (23 x 20 threads)

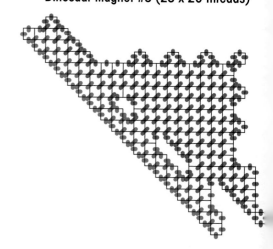

10

Beboppin' Numbers

You can "count" on these dancing number magnets to make amusing teaching tools for youngsters. Their kooky expressions make learning especially fun.

BEBOPPIN' NUMBERS

Size: 4¹/₂"w x 6¹/₂"h each

Supplies: Worsted weight yarn (refer to color key and photo), one 10¹/₂" x 13¹/₂" sheet of 7 mesh plastic canvas, #16 tapestry needle, two 12mm moving eyes, two 6" lengths of 6mm black chenille stems, ¹/₄" pom-pom, 3" of ¹/₄"w satin ribbon, fine-tooth comb, sewing thread, magnetic strip, and craft glue.

Stitches used: Backstitch, French Knot, Fringe Stitch, Overcast Stitch, and Tent Stitch.

Instructions: Referring to photo for yarn colors, follow charts to cut and stitch desired magnet pieces, working backstitches and fringe stitches last. For hair, separate each strand of fringe into plies. Use fine-tooth comb to comb fringe until the desired look is achieved. For arms and legs, refer to photo and insert chenille stems through stitched piece. Glue one Hand to each arm. Glue one Foot to each leg. For bow, fold ribbon length into thirds and wrap center with matching sewing thread. Glue eyes, pom-pom, and bow to magnet. Glue magnetic strip to back of magnet.

Designs by Jack Peatman for LuvLee Designs.

	COLOR
✎	white
✎	red
✎	black
✎	number color
●	red Fr. knot
◉	optional color fringe

Hand A
(6 x 5 threads)

Hand B
(6 x 5 threads)

Foot A
(7 x 5 threads)

Foot B
(7 x 5 threads)

1 (11 x 24 threads)

2 (17 x 24 threads)

3 (17 x 24 threads)

4 (20 x 24 threads)

5 (17 x 24 threads)

6 (17 x 24 threads)

7 (17 x 24 threads)

8 (15 x 24 threads)

9 (17 x 24 threads)

0 (15 x 24 threads)

Sew-Easy Magnets

For a quick gift idea that's "sew" easy to make, simply fashion our spool magnet in different colors and pair it with our scissors. Anyone who loves to stitch will think you're on the cutting edge of gift giving!

SEW-EASY MAGNETS

Approx. size: 2"w x 3"h each
Supplies: Worsted weight yarn or Needloff® Plastic Canvas Yarn (refer to color key), one 10½" x 13½" sheet of 7 mesh plastic canvas, #16 tapestry needle, magnetic strip, and craft glue.
For Spool: Additional #16 tapestry needle.
For Scissors: Black embroidery floss.

Stitches used: Backstitch, Gobelin Stitch, Overcast Stitch, and Tent Stitch.
Instructions: Follow chart to cut and stitch desired magnet, working backstitches last. Glue magnetic strip to back of magnet.

For Spool: Cut a 4½" length of match yarn. Thread yarn through needle. Refer photo to place needle under yarn on Spo

Designs by Peggy Astle.

COLOR (NL)
turquoise (50)
tan (16)
grey (38)
thread color
*black embroidery floss

*Use 6 strands of floss.

Spool
(13 x 17 threads)

Scissors
(14 x 24 threads)

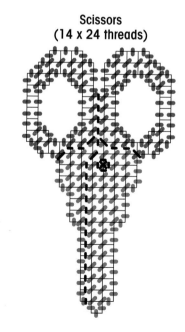

A Year of Flowers

*Abloom with color, these magnets depict a full year of pretty florals.
Display them as a set or enjoy a new blossom each month. The pretty
posies are also just the right size to make cheery plant pokes.*

A YEAR OF FLOWERS

Approx. size: 3¹⁄₂" x 3¹⁄₄" each

Supplies: Worsted weight yarn or Needloft® Plastic Canvas Yarn and DMC embroidery floss (refer to color key), one 10¹⁄₂" x 13¹⁄₂" sheet of 7 mesh plastic canvas, #16 tapestry needle, magnetic strip, and craft glue.

Stitches used: Backstitch, Overcast Stitch, and Tent Stitch.

Instructions: Follow chart to cut and stitch desired magnet, using six strands of embroidery floss and working backstitches last. Using white overcast stitches, cover unworked edges. Glue magnetic strip to back of magnet.

Designs by Jorja Hernandez.

YARN (NL)	FLOSS (DMC)
white (41)	orange (900)
ecru (39)	dk pink (309)
lt yellow (19)	red (304)
yellow (57)	purple (327)
gold (11)	blue (825)
orange (12)	green (562)
dk orange (52)	rust (3777)
peach (47)	
lt pink (08)	
pink (07)	
dk pink (55)	
red (02)	
dk red (42)	
lt purple (44)	
purple (59)	
dk purple (46)	
lt blue (36)	
blue (35)	
blue green (53)	
lime (22)	
olive (24)	
lt green (25)	
green (23)	
dk green (27)	

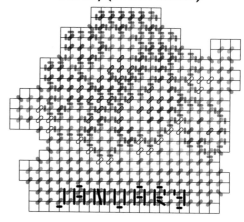

January (24 x 21 threads)

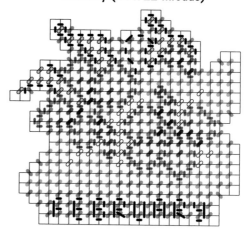

February (24 x 22 threads)

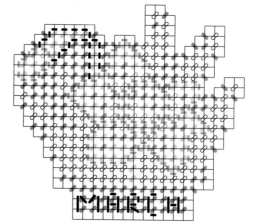

March (24 x 22 threads)

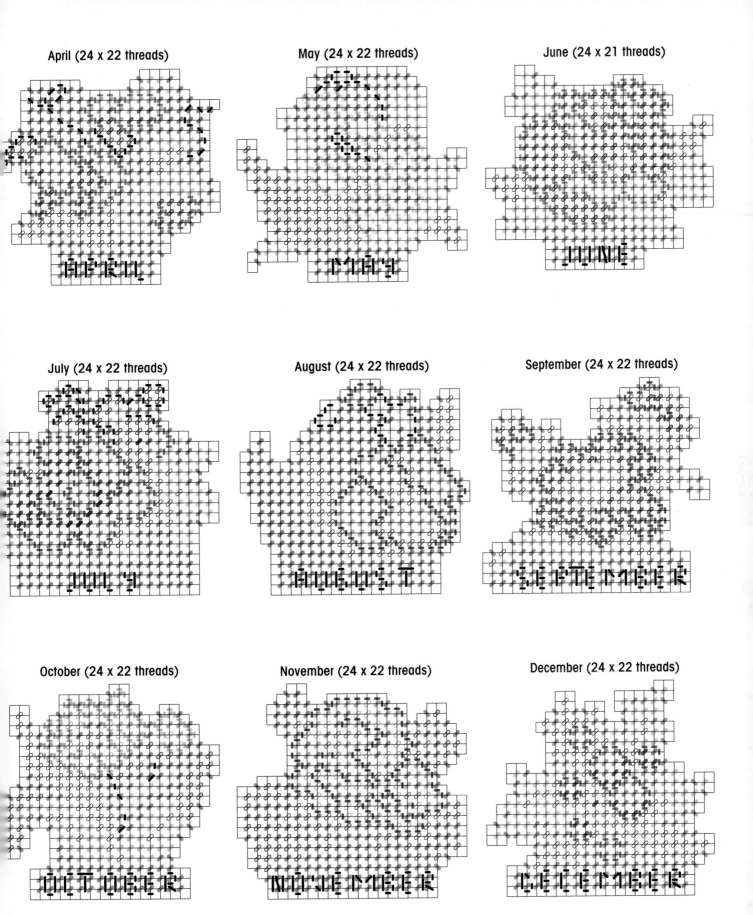

April (24 x 22 threads)

May (24 x 22 threads)

June (24 x 21 threads)

July (24 x 22 threads)

August (24 x 22 threads)

September (24 x 22 threads)

October (24 x 22 threads)

November (24 x 22 threads)

December (24 x 22 threads)

Old-timey Magnets

Fashioned with an air of nostalgia, these magnets portray images of simple country life — a wood-burning stove, a jar of strawberry jam, a bean jar, a well-worn washboard, and other timeless images.

OLD-TIMEY MAGNETS

Approx. size: 3"w x 3"h each

Supplies: DMC embroidery floss (refer to color keys), one 10½" x 13½" sheet of 10 mesh plastic canvas, #20 tapestry needle, magnetic strip, and craft glue.

Stitches used: Backstitch, French Knot, Overcast Stitch, and Tent Stitch.

Instructions: Follow chart to cut and stitch desired magnet, working backstitches and French knots last and using twelve strands of floss unless otherwise noted. Glue magnetic strip to back of magnet.

Designs by Maryanne Moreck.

COLOR (DMC)	COLOR (DMC)	COLOR (DMC)
white (blanc)	lt blue (932)	black (310)
ecru (739)	blue (931)	*brown (433)
gold (729)	lt green (320)	*black (310)
pink (760)	green (319)	brown Fr. knot (433)
dk pink (3328)	lt brown (436)	black Fr. knot (310)
red (347)	brown (433)	*Use 6 strands of floss.

Bed and Board (31 x 19 threads)

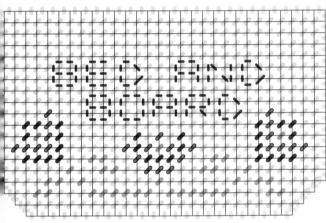

Eggs (26 x 22 threads)

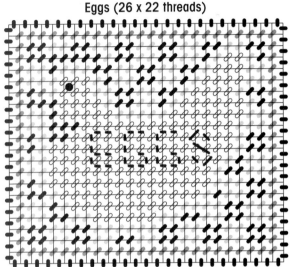

Flower Basket (25 x 21 threads)

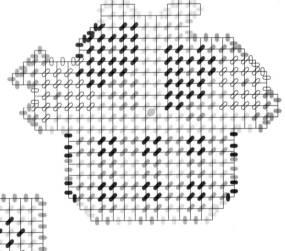

Home Sweet Home (27 x 19 threads)

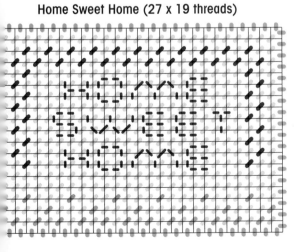

Bean Jar (19 x 27 threads)

19

House (27 x 21 threads)

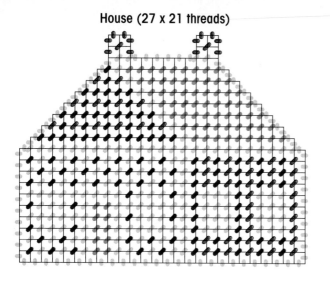

Wanted (27 x 24 threads)

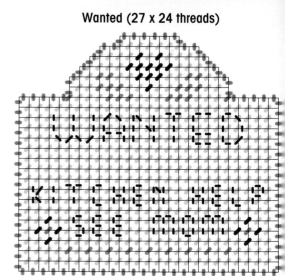

Heart (26 x 21 threads)

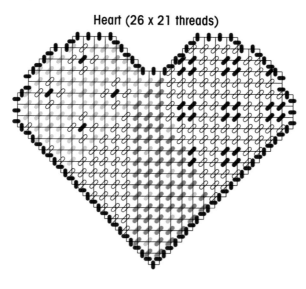

Clock (19 x 30 threads)

Stove (21 x 30 threads)

Washboard (17 x 27 threads)

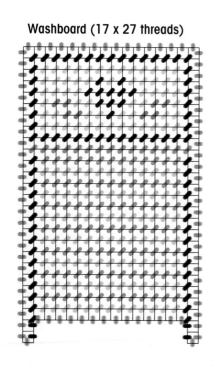

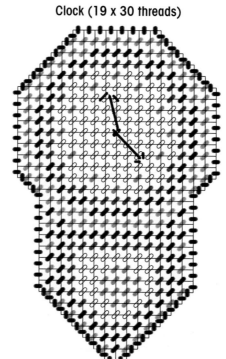

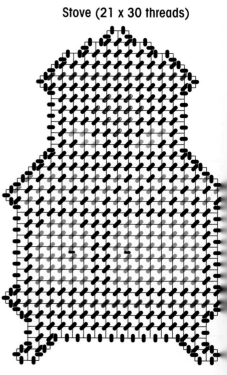

20

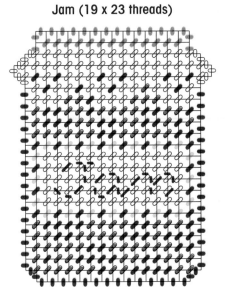

Jam (19 x 23 threads)

COLOR (DMC)	COLOR (DMC)	COLOR (DMC)
white (blanc)	blue (931)	grey (535)
ecru (739)	dk blue (3750)	black (310)
gold (729)	lt green (320)	*black (310)
pink (760)	green (319)	black Fr. knot (310)
dk pink (3328)	lt brown (436)	*Use 6 strands of floss.
red (347)	brown (433)	
lt blue (932)	lt grey (647)	

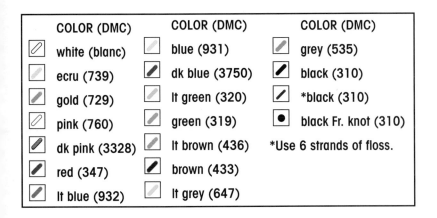

Cat (33 x 20 threads)

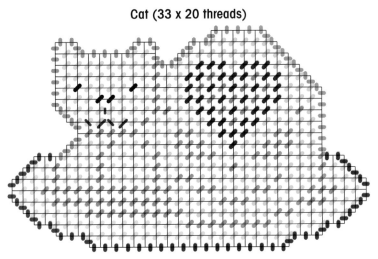

Sewing Machine (27 x 19 threads)

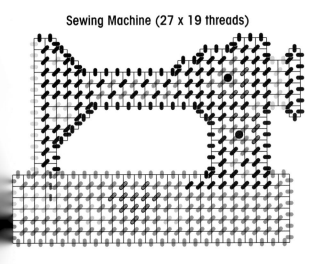

Dutch Oven (32 x 21 threads)

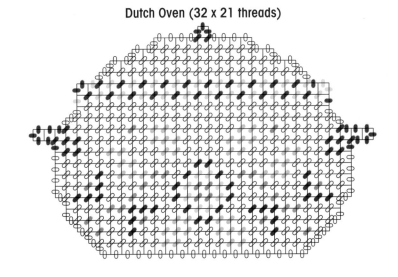

Dandy Dice

You'll be a high roller with these fun magnets holding up your notes! Whether displayed as a set or paired in lucky sevens, one thing's for sure: these cute stick-ups make a winning ensemble!

DANDY DICE

Size: 1¹/₂"w x 1¹/₂"h each

Supplies: Worsted weight yarn or Needloft® Plastic Canvas Yarn (refer to color key), one 10¹/₂" x 13¹/₂" sheet of 7 mesh plastic canvas, #16 tapestry needle, magnetic strip, and craft glue.

Stitches used: French Knot, Overcast Stitch, and Tent Stitch.

Instructions: Follow chart to cut and stitch desired magnet, working French knots last. Using white overcast stitches, cover unworked edges. Glue magnetic strip to back of magnet.

Designs by L.R. Thompson.

	COLOR (NL)
✎	white (41)
•	black (00) Fr. knot

#1 (10 x 10 threads)

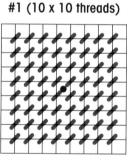

#2 (10 x 10 threads)

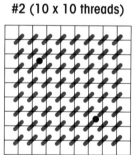

#3 (10 x 10 threads)

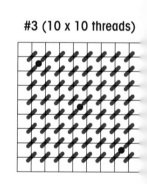

#4 (10 x 10 threads)

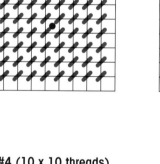

#5 (10 x 10 threads)

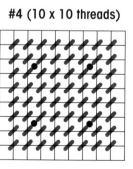

#6 (10 x 10 threads)

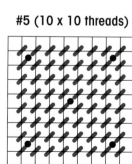

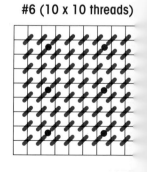

Dancing Veggies

You can't "beet" this magnetic set for adding variety to your message center! The garden-fresh crew features a cast of crispy characters to remind you to eat your veggies.

NCING VEGGIES

prox. size: 5"w x 7 1/2"h each

pplies: Worsted weight yarn (refer to or key), one 10 1/2" x 13 1/2" sheet of mesh plastic canvas, #16 tapestry dle, two 10mm moving eyes, one 5mm en pom-pom, one 12" 3mm black nille stem, magnetic strip, and craft e.

Stitches used: Backstitch, Gobelin Stitch, Overcast Stitch, Reversed Tent Stitch, and Tent Stitch.

Instructions: Follow charts to cut and stitch desired magnet pieces, working backstitches last. Refer to photo to glue eyes and pom-pom to magnet. Tie an 8" length of yarn in a bow; trim ends. Refer to photo to glue bow to magnet. For arms and legs, cut two 6" lengths of chenille stem.

Thread ends of one chenille stem through magnet from back to front for arms. Repeat for legs. Glue Hands and Feet to arms and legs; shape as desired. Glue magnetic strip to back of magnet.

Designs by Jack Peatman for LuvLee Designs.

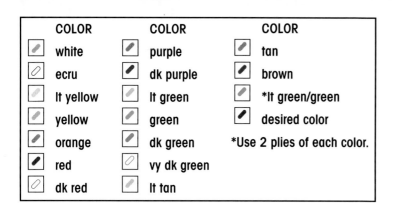

COLOR	COLOR	COLOR
white	purple	tan
ecru	dk purple	brown
lt yellow	lt green	*lt green/green
yellow	green	desired color
orange	dk green	*Use 2 plies of each color.
red	vy dk green	
dk red	lt tan	

Hands (6 x 7 threads each)

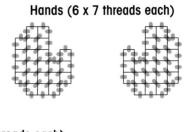

Feet (9 x 5 threads each)

Beet (18 x 28 threads)

Green Pepper (19 x 26 threads)

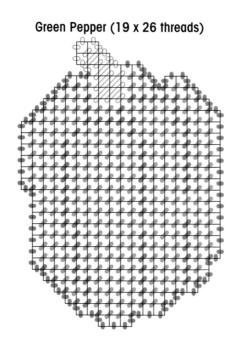

Turnip (20 x 28 threads)

Radish (20 x 28 threads)

Cucumber (15 x 29 threads)

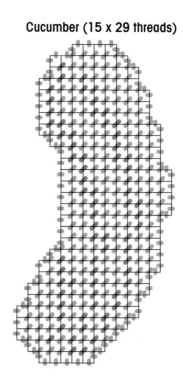

Eggplant (19 x 30 threads)

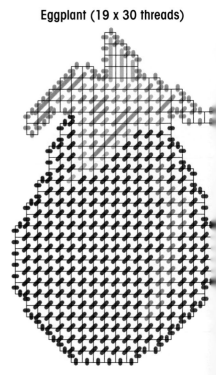

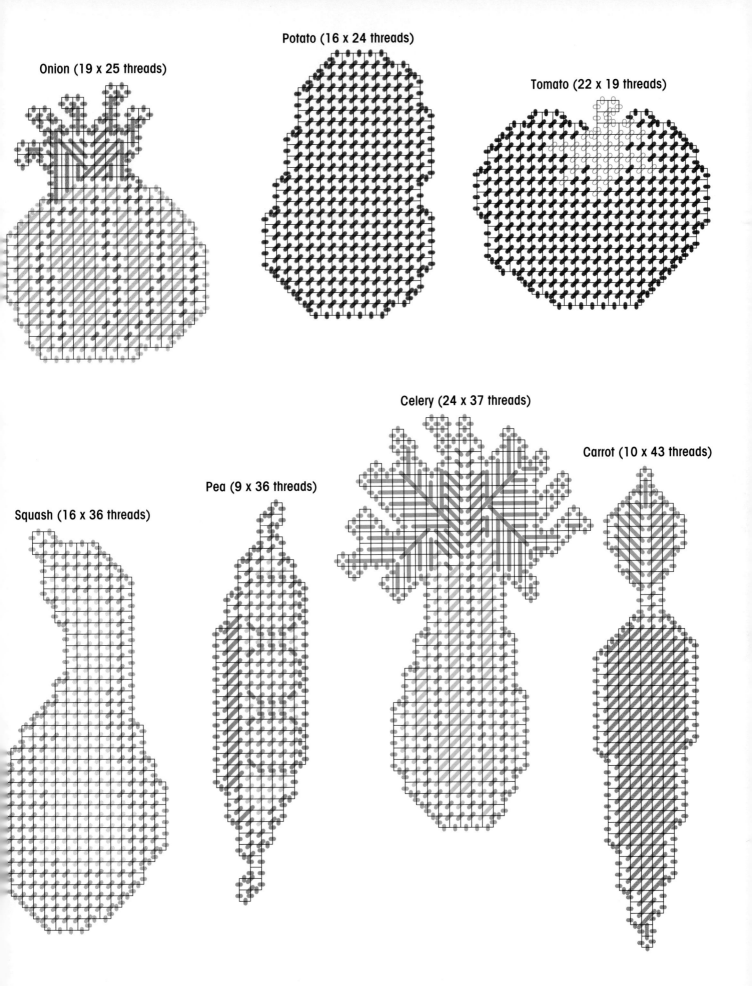

Onion (19 x 25 threads)

Potato (16 x 24 threads)

Tomato (22 x 19 threads)

Squash (16 x 36 threads)

Pea (9 x 36 threads)

Celery (24 x 37 threads)

Carrot (10 x 43 threads)

Road Signs

Stop! Yield! One way! Our playful road sign magnets will certainly call attention to all your notes and reminders. The miniature speed limit sign will also make an amusing gift for a lead-footed friend!

OAD SIGNS

prox. size: 2³/₄"w x 3¹/₄"h each

pplies: Worsted weight yarn or Needloft® stic Canvas Yarn (refer to color key), e 10¹/₂" x 13¹/₂" sheet of 7 mesh plastic nvas, #16 tapestry needle, magnetic p, and craft glue.

tches used: Backstitch, Cross Stitch, ercast Stitch, Reversed Tent Stitch, and t Stitch.

tructions: Follow chart to cut and stitch sired magnet, working backstitches last. e magnetic strip to back of magnet.

signs by Karen Hanley.

Stop (20 x 19 threads)

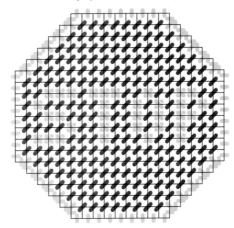

	COLOR (NL)
	white (41)
	yellow (57)
	red (02)
	green (27)
	black (00)

Traffic Light (11 x 21 threads)

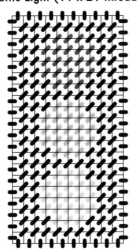

One Way (14 x 22 threads)

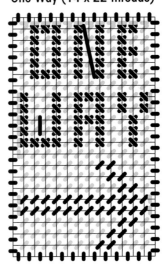

Speed Limit (18 x 25 threads)

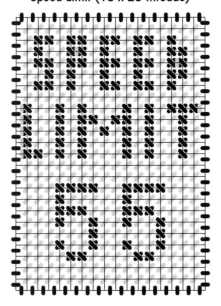

Yield (30 x 24 threads)

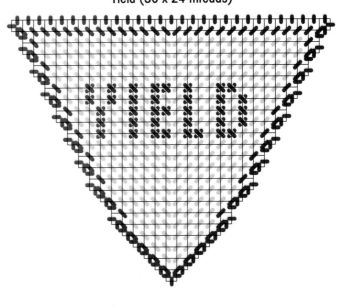

Summertime Favorites

Sweet sentiments of summer will linger year-round with these adorable little magnets. They'll brighten notes, artwork, photographs, or anything else you choose to display.

Labor Day Cookout Sat. 6:00 pm

watermelon tomatoes strawberries apples

UMMERTIME FAVORITES

prox. size: 1³/₄"w x 2"h each

pplies: Worsted weight yarn or Needloft® astic Canvas Yarn (refer to color key), e 10¹/₂" x 13¹/₂" sheet of 7 mesh plastic nvas, #16 tapestry needle, magnetic ip, and craft glue.

r Ladybug only: One 3" length of black oth-covered floral wire.

r Flag only: Kreinik metallic gold (002) "w ribbon.

tches used: Backstitch, French Knot, belin Stitch, Overcast Stitch, and Tent tch.

structions: Follow chart to cut and stitch sired magnet, working backstitches and ench knots last. Referring to photo for rn color, cover unworked edges. Glue agnetic strip to back of magnet.

r Ladybug only: Referring to photo, bend ral wire to form antennae. Glue floral wire back of Ladybug.

g and Hot Air Balloon designs by Ann amlet.

dybug and Watermelon designs by gy Astle.

nbrella design by Barbara C. eitwieser.

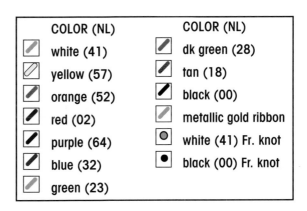

COLOR (NL)	COLOR (NL)
white (41)	dk green (28)
yellow (57)	tan (18)
orange (52)	black (00)
red (02)	metallic gold ribbon
purple (64)	white (41) Fr. knot
blue (32)	black (00) Fr. knot
green (23)	

Flag (15 x 14 threads)

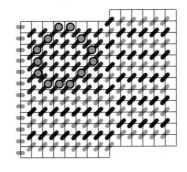

Hot Air Balloon (13 x 18 threads)

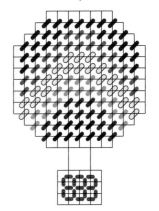

Ladybug (10 x 13 threads)

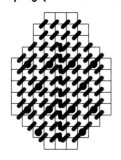

Umbrella (12 x 15 threads)

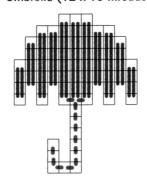

Watermelon (14 x 9 threads)

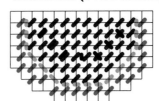

29

Back to Nature

From the blissful sun to a radiant rainbow, nature's beauty shines in this cheery assortment. Some of God's smallest and most whimsical creatures share the limelight, too!

BACK TO NATURE

Approx. size: 3¹/₂"w x 3¹/₄"h each

Supplies: Worsted weight yarn (refer to color key), one 10¹/₂" x 13¹/₂" sheet of 7 mesh plastic canvas, #16 tapestry needle, magnetic strip, and craft glue.

For Bee and Butterfly: 6" length of 3mm black chenille stem.

Stitches used: Backstitch, Cross Stitch, French Knot, Gobelin Stitch, Mosaic Stitch, Overcast Stitch, Scotch Stitch, and Tent Stitch.

Instructions: Follow chart(s) to cut and stitch desired magnet piece(s), working backstitches and French knots last. Glue magnetic strip to back of magnet.

For Bee and Butterfly: For antennae, cut chenille stem in half. Referring to photo, glue chenille stem pieces to back of magnet. Shape and trim antennae.

For Daisy: Referring to photo, glue Daisy Center to Daisy Base.

Designs by Dick Martin.

COLOR		COLOR		COLOR	
▧	white	▨	blue	▨	black
▨	ecru		lt green	▨	*lt orange
▨	lt yellow		green	▨	*pink
▨	yellow	▨	dk green	▨	*black
▨	lt orange		lt olive	●	*white Fr. knot
▨	orange		olive	●	*yellow Fr. knot
▨	lt pink		lt tan	●	*lt blue Fr. knot
▨	pink	▨	brown	●	*black Fr. knot
▨	red	▨	dk brown		*Use 2 plies of yarn.

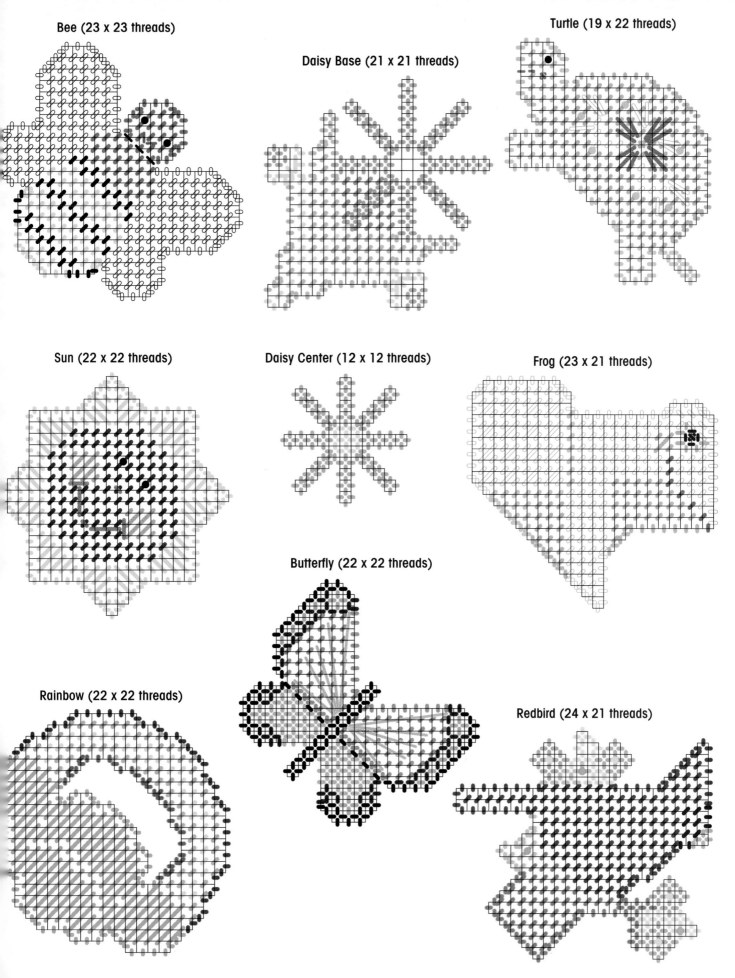

Bee (23 x 23 threads)

Turtle (19 x 22 threads)

Daisy Base (21 x 21 threads)

Sun (22 x 22 threads)

Daisy Center (12 x 12 threads)

Frog (23 x 21 threads)

Butterfly (22 x 22 threads)

Rainbow (22 x 22 threads)

Redbird (24 x 21 threads)

Barnyard Buddies

If farm living is the life for you, then you'll want to add these barnyard buddies to your magnet collection. The classic country characters will add down-home charm to your message center.

ARNYARD BUDDIES

prox. size: 2"w x 2"h each

upplies: Worsted weight yarn or Needloft® astic Canvas yarn (refer to color key), one 0½" x 13½" sheet of 7 mesh plastic nvas, #16 tapestry needle, magnetic ip, and craft glue.

tches used: Backstitch, Gobelin Stitch, ercast Stitch, and Tent Stitch.

structions:

r Cow, follow chart to cut and stitch Cow. ue magnetic strip to back of magnet.

r Chicken, follow charts to cut and stitch icken pieces. Matching ★'s and ■'s and ing white yarn, join Wings to Chicken ong unworked edges. Glue magnetic strip back of magnet.

r Pig, follow charts to cut and stitch Pig ces, working backstitches last. Matching s and ▼'s and using pink yarn, join Ears Face along unworked edges. Referring to oto, tack Nose to Face. Glue magnetic p to back of magnet.

signs by MizFitz.

COLOR (NL)	
⬜	white (41)
⬜	yellow (57)
⬜	peach (56)
⬜	pink (07)
⬜	red (01)
✎	black (00)

Cow (18 x 14 threads)

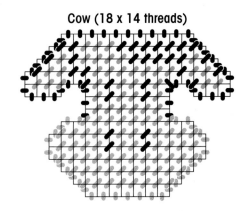

Pig Face (13 x 13 threads)

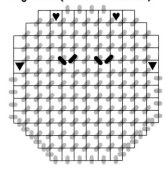

Chicken Wing
x 9 threads)

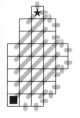

Chicken Wing
(6 x 9 threads)

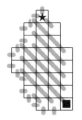

Chicken (13 x 19 threads)

Pig Nose (5 x 5 threads)

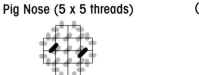

Pig Ear
(5 x 6 threads)

Pig Ear
(5 x 6 threads)

33

Delicious Temptations

To satisfy your sweet tooth, try posting these tasty-looking magnets on the refrigerator — instead of sampling the delicious temptations inside.

DELICIOUS TEMPTATIONS

Approx. size: 3"w x 3"h each

Supplies: Worsted weight yarn (refer to color keys), one 10½" x 13½" sheet of mesh plastic canvas, #16 tapestry needle, magnetic strip, and craft glue.

For Candy Cluster: Plastic wrap and black yarn.

Stitches used: Backstitch, Cross Stitch, French Knot, Gobelin Stitch, Overcast Stitch, Tent Stitch, and Turkey Loop Stitch.

Instructions: Follow chart(s) to cut and stitch desired magnet piece(s), working Backstitches, French knots, and Turkey Loops last. Glue magnetic strip to back of magnet.

For Banana Split, glue Cherry to Banana Split.

For Candy Cluster, wrap Candy #4 and Candy #5 in plastic wrap; secure ends with black yarn. Glue all Candy pieces together before gluing magnetic strip to back.

Designs by Jack Peatman for LuvLee Designs.

COLOR		COLOR		COLOR	
	white		green		orange Fr. knot
	ecru		dk green		dk pink Fr. knot
	yellow		tan		red Fr. knot
	gold		dk brown		lt blue Fr. knot
	lt pink		grey		green Fr. knot
	pink		*blue		white Turkey loop
	rose		*dk green		*Use 2 plies of yarn.
	red		ecru Fr. knot		
	lt blue		yellow Fr. knot		

Hoagie (33 x 17 threads)

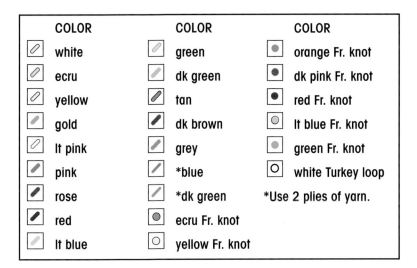

Gingerbread Man (21 x 25 threads)

Ice-Cream Soda (19 x 28 threads)

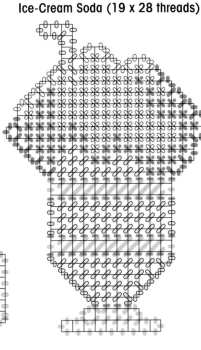

Ice-Cream Cone (16 x 28 threads)

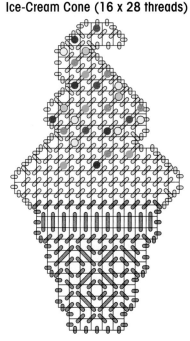

Butterscotch Pudding (31 x 20 threads)

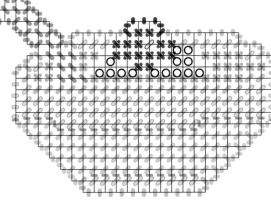

Chocolates (30 x 17 threads)

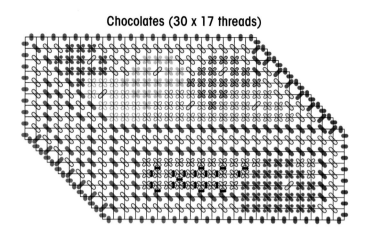

Chocolate Cake (22 x 20 threads)

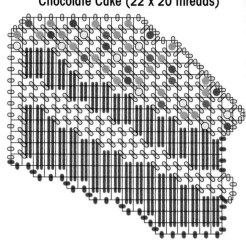

Potato Chips (21 x 22 threads)

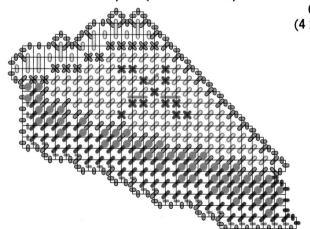

Donut (24 x 21 threads)

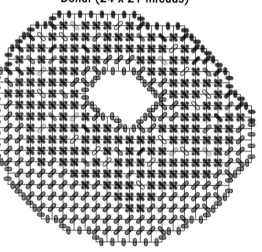

Popsicle® (14 x 35 threads)

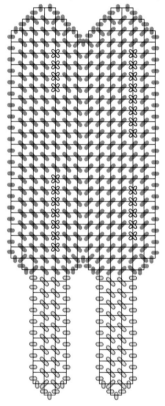

Blueberry Pie (27 x 20 threads)

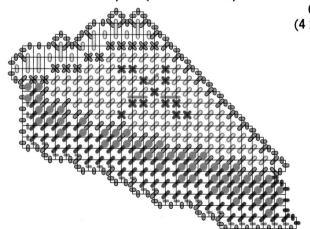

Candy #1
(4 x 4 threads)

Candy #2
(4 x 4 threads)

Candy #3 (16 x 11 threads)

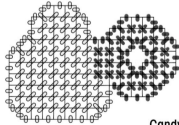

Candy #4
(8 x 8 threads)

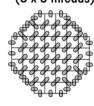

Candy #5
(11 x 5 threads)

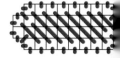

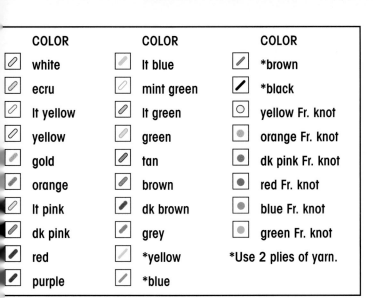

COLOR	COLOR	COLOR
white	lt blue	*brown
ecru	mint green	*black
lt yellow	lt green	yellow Fr. knot
yellow	green	orange Fr. knot
gold	tan	dk pink Fr. knot
orange	brown	red Fr. knot
lt pink	dk brown	blue Fr. knot
dk pink	grey	green Fr. knot
red	*yellow	*Use 2 plies of yarn.
purple	*blue	

Gelatin (28 x 29 threads)

Cherry (4 x 4 threads)

Banana Split (28 x 14 threads)

Ice Cream On A Stick
(17 x 33 threads)

Onion Rings (26 x 21 threads)

Caramel Apple (19 x 25 threads)

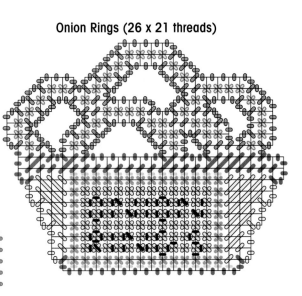

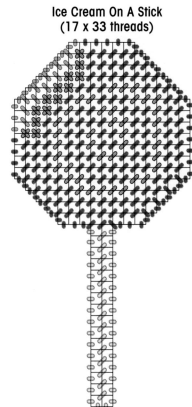

Positive Rewards

These little magnets are big on praise! Post them with children's schoolwork, or tuck them in a lunch box for a midday surprise. Why not add a safety pin to the back of the gold star for a "good job" badge they'll be proud to wear!

POSITIVE REWARDS

Approx. size: 4"w x 3"h each
Supplies: Worsted weight yarn (refer to color key), one 10½" x 13½" sheet of 7 mesh plastic canvas, #16 tapestry needle, magnetic strip, and craft glue.
For Gold Star: Kreinik ⅛"w metallic gold ribbon.

Stitches used: Backstitch, Cross Stitch, French Knot, Mosaic Stitch, Overcast Stitch, and Tent Stitch.
Instructions: Follow charts to cut and stitch desired magnet pieces, working lettering backstitches and French knots last. Glue magnetic strip to back of magnet.

For WE LOVE IT!: Refer to photo and orange to tack Mom to We Love It! green to tack Dad to We Love It!

Designs by Dick Martin.

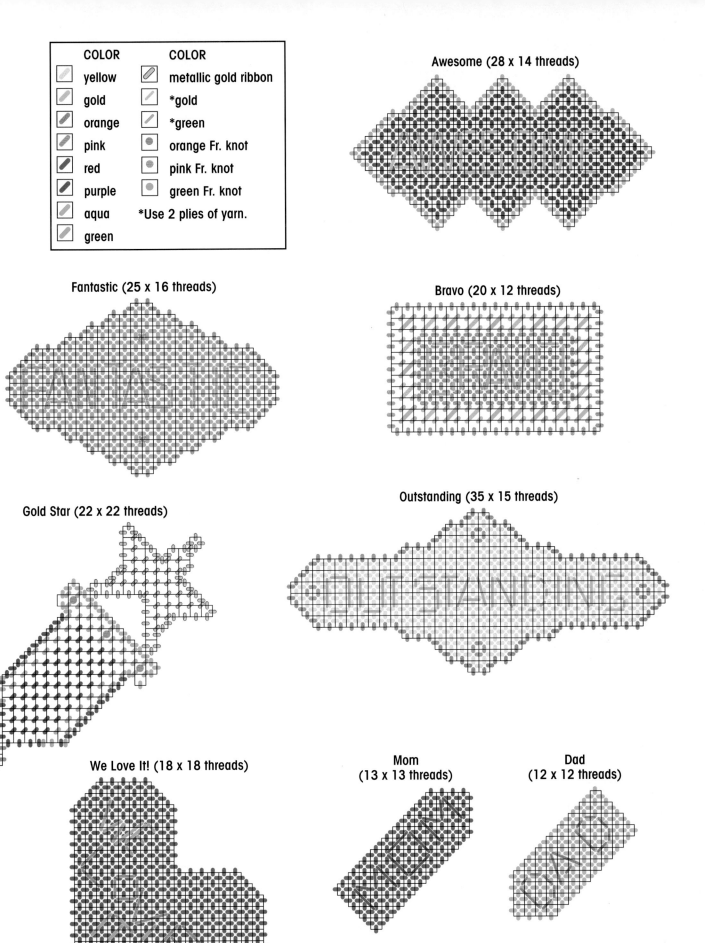

COLOR		COLOR	
	yellow		metallic gold ribbon
	gold		*gold
	orange		*green
	pink		orange Fr. knot
	red		pink Fr. knot
	purple		green Fr. knot
	aqua	*Use 2 plies of yarn.	
	green		

Awesome (28 x 14 threads)

Fantastic (25 x 16 threads)

Bravo (20 x 12 threads)

Gold Star (22 x 22 threads)

Outstanding (35 x 15 threads)

We Love It! (18 x 18 threads)

Mom
(13 x 13 threads)

Dad
(12 x 12 threads)

"Classy" Work

Back to school means homework, and students will love displaying their best papers with our four magnets. These colorful little projects also make thoughtful tokens to let special teachers know how much they're appreciated.

"CLASSY" WORK

Approx. size: 3¼"w x 3"h each

Supplies: Worsted weight yarn or Needloft® Plastic Canvas Yarn (refer to color key), one 10½" x 13½" sheet of 7 mesh plastic canvas, #16 tapestry needle, magnetic strip, and craft glue.

For Pencil: White/silver cord.

For Schoolhouse: One ³⁄₈" gold liberty bell and one 6" length of ¹⁄₈"w white ribbon.

Stitches used: Backstitch, Gobelin Stitch, Overcast Stitch, Reversed Tent Stitch, and Tent Stitch.

Instructions: Follow chart(s) to cut and stitch desired magnet piece(s), completing background with black tent stitches as indicated on chart and working backstitches last. Glue magnetic strip to back of magnet.

For Apple, refer to photo to glue Apple Leaf to apple.

For Schoolhouse, thread ribbon through bell and tie a bow. Trim ribbon ends. Refer to photo to glue bow with bell to Schoolhouse.

Designs by Peggy Astle.

	COLOR (NL)
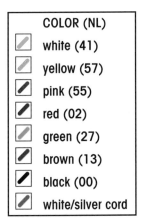	white (41)
	yellow (57)
	pink (55)
	red (02)
	green (27)
	brown (13)
	black (00)
	white/silver cord

Apple Leaf (8 x 6 threads)

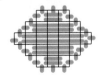

Apple (16 x 17 threads)

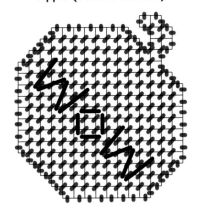

Pencil (31 x 10 threads)

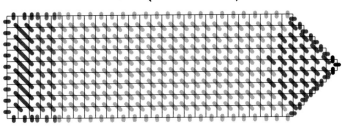

Slate (20 x 26 threads)

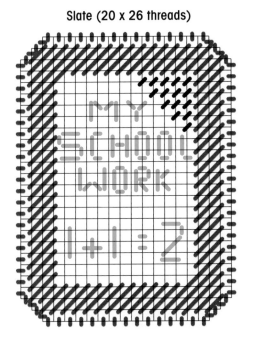

Schoolhouse (20 x 27 threads)

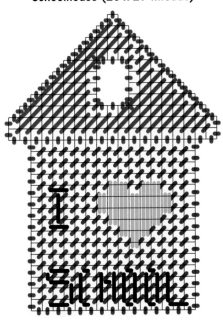

"Zoo-pendous" Pals

These "zoo-pendous" characters have loads of magnetic charm! Ready to munch on their favorite snacks, our curious monkey and amusing elephant will be great for displaying snapshots, school papers, and more.

"ZOO-PENDOUS" PALS

Approx. size: 4"w x 3³/₄"h each

Supplies: Worsted weight yarn (refer to color key), one 10¹/₂" x 13¹/₂" sheet of 7 mesh plastic canvas, #16 tapestry needle, magnetic strip, and craft glue.

For Elephant: Two 4.5mm blue animal eyes.

For Monkey: Two 10mm brown animal eyes.

Stitches used: Backstitch, Cross Stitch, Gobelin Stitch, Overcast Stitch, and Tent Stitch.

Instructions: Follow charts to cut and stitch desired magnet pieces, working backstitches last. Referring to photo, glue eyes to Head; glue pieces together. Glue magnetic strip to back of magnet.

Designs by Darla J. Fanton.

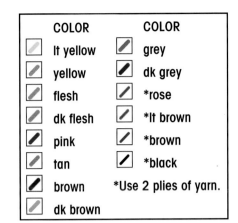

COLOR		COLOR	
	lt yellow		grey
	yellow		dk grey
	flesh		*rose
	dk flesh		*lt brown
	pink		*brown
	tan		*black
	brown		*Use 2 plies of yarn.
	dk brown		

Foot (6 x 6 threads)
(stitch 2)

Elephant Head (20 x 18 threads)

Peanut (20 x 20 threads)

Paw (4 x 4 threads)
(stitch 2)

Monkey Head (15 x 15 threads)

Banana (26 x 21 threads)

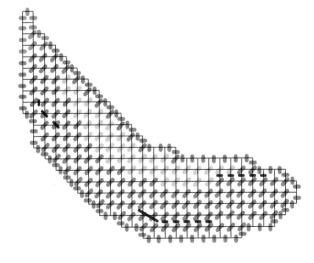

43

Native American Mandala

Steeped in culture, the ancient mandala is a classic symbol of the rich heritage of Native Americans. Traditionally, the shield's hoop circle, which represents the never-ending balance of life, is decorated with images that hold significance to the owner.

NATIVE AMERICAN MANDALA

Size: 3"w x 6¼"h

Supplies: Worsted weight yarn (refer to color key), one Darice 3" dia. plastic canvas circle, #16 tapestry needle, six 5mm x 7mm red wood beads, six 10mm brown wood beads, one 16mm brown wood bead, 6" length of string, fine-tooth comb, magnetic strip, and craft glue.

Stitches used: Backstitch, Cross Stitch, Fringe Stitch, Gobelin Stitch, and Overcast Stitch.

Instructions: Follow chart to cut and stitch magnet, working fringe stitches last. Use two 16" lengths of yarn to work each fringe stitch. Separate each strand of fringe into plies. Comb plies until the desired look is achieved. Referring to photo, thread fringe through brown beads. Trim ends of fringe from 2½" to 3½". Tie a knot close to one end of 6" length of string. Thread remaining end through three red beads, tying knots between beads to separate. Thread loose end of string through Mandala at ■'s. Thread end through remaining red beads, tying knots between beads to separate. Tie a knot close to end of string; trim ends. Glue magnetic strip to back of magnet.

Design by Shirley M. Wiskow.

COLOR	COLOR
white	grey
ecru	*white fringe
gold	*gold fringe
tan	*dk brown fringe
brown	*grey fringe
dk brown	*Use 2 strands of yarn.

Mandala

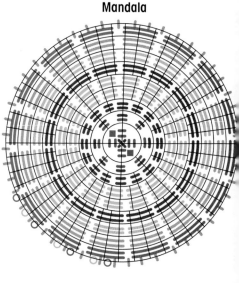

44

Zodiac Signs

With this collection of astrological signs at your fingertips, you'll have a treasure-trove of quick gift ideas for all your friends with magnetic personalities!

ZODIAC SIGNS

Approx. size: 3³/₄" x 3³/₄" each

Supplies: Worsted weight yarn or Needloft® Plastic Canvas Yarn and DMC embroidery floss (refer to color key), one 10¹/₂" x 13¹/₂" sheet of 7 mesh plastic canvas, #16 tapestry needle, magnetic strip, and craft glue.

Stitches used: Backstitch, Cross Stitch, French Knot, Overcast Stitch, and Tent Stitch.

Instructions: Follow chart to cut and stitch desired magnet, working backstitches and French knots last. Referring to photo for color, use overcast stitches to cover unworked edges. Glue magnetic strip to back of magnet.

Designs by Holly Defount .

COLOR (NL)	COLOR (NL)	COLOR (NL)
white (41)	burgundy (42)	lt grey (37)
vy lt yellow (21)	purple (45)	grey (38)
lt yellow (20)	lt blue (36)	black (00)
yellow (19)	blue (34)	royal blue (32) Fr. knot
dk yellow (57)	dk blue (33)	**FLOSS (DMC)**
gold (11)	royal blue (32)	yellow (727)
dk gold (17)	navy (48)	plum (3685)
orange (12)	lt aqua (49)	lt blue (597)
peach (47)	aqua (54)	blue (806)
lt pink (08)	green (27)	dk blue (3750)
pink (07)	rust (09)	lt brown (434)
dk pink (55)	beige (40)	brown (400)
red (02)	tan (43)	grey (535)
dk red (01)	brown (15)	black (310)

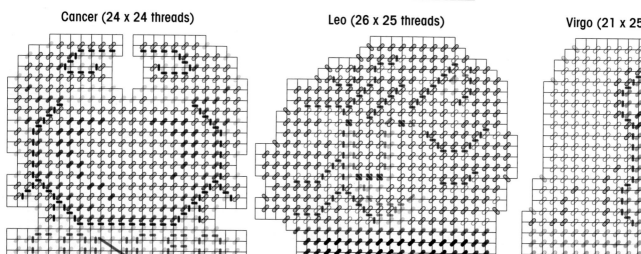

Aries (20 x 25 threads)

Taurus (24 x 26 threads)

Gemini (25 x 24 threads)

Cancer (24 x 24 threads)

Leo (26 x 25 threads)

Virgo (21 x 25 threads)

Libra (24 x 24 threads)

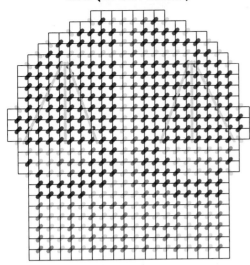

Scorpio (25 x 23 threads)

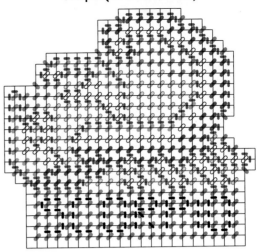

Sagittarius (30 x 26 threads)

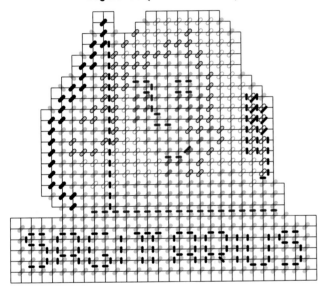

Capricorn (26 x 25 threads)

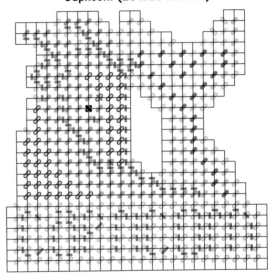

Aquarius (26 x 24 threads)

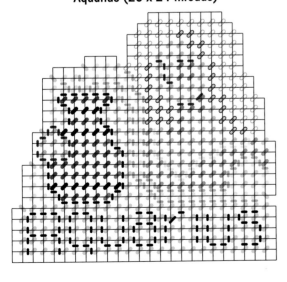

Pisces (25 x 24 threads)

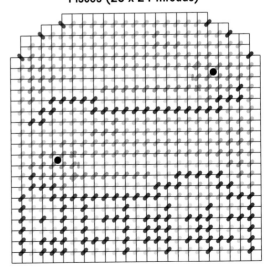

Meow Mix

These cute magnets are the cat's meow! Fashion just the felines that catch your fancy, or complete them all for a collection that's beyond "purr-fection."

MEOW MIX

approx. size: 2½"w x 3½"h each

Supplies: Worsted weight yarn and embroidery floss (refer to color keys), one 10½" x 13½" sheet of 7 mesh plastic canvas, #16 tapestry needle, #24 tapestry needle, magnetic strip, and craft glue.

Stitches used: Backstitch, French Knot, Gobelin Stitch, Overcast Stitch, Reversed Tent Stitch, and Tent Stitch.

Instructions: Follow chart to cut and stitch desired magnet, working backstitches and French knots last. Glue magnetic strip to back of magnet.

For Mischa and Peaches: For each bow, tie an 8" length of yarn in a bow; trim ends. Glue bow to magnet.

For Dumplin', Sophie, Sylvester, Buster, Benjamin, and Pepper: For each bow, thread an 8" length of yarn through Magnet ▲'s; tie yarn in a bow. Trim ends.

For Jasmine, Tinkerbell, Twinkie, Yoda, Dan, Bootsie, Elvis, Smokey, and Prissy: For each bow, tie an 8" length of yarn in a bow around cat's neck; trim ends.

Designs by Dick Martin.

	COLOR
✎	white
✎	lt pink
✎	pink
✎	green
✎	tan
✎	grey
✎	black
●	*green Fr. knot
●	*black Fr. knot
*Use 2 plies of yarn.	
	COLOR
✎	†white
✎	†black
†Use 2 strands of floss.	

Smokey (19 x 20 threads)

Buster & Benjamin (28 x 22 threads)

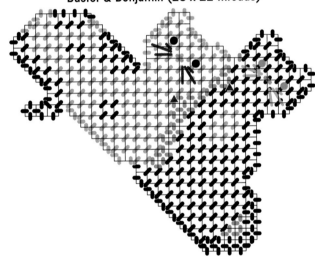

Mischa (21 x 21 threads)

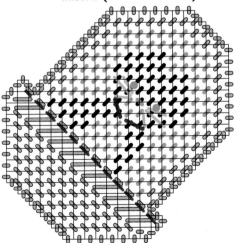

Jasmine (22 x 19 threads)

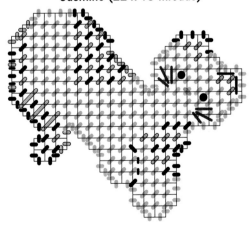

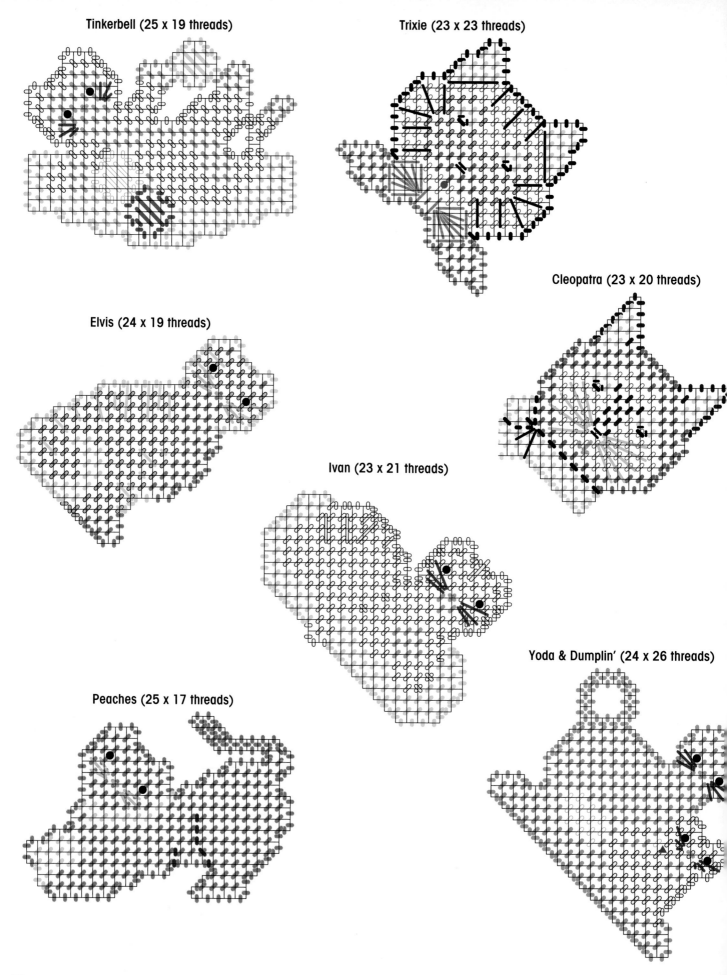

Tinkerbell (25 x 19 threads)

Trixie (23 x 23 threads)

Cleopatra (23 x 20 threads)

Elvis (24 x 19 threads)

Ivan (23 x 21 threads)

Yoda & Dumplin' (24 x 26 threads)

Peaches (25 x 17 threads)

50

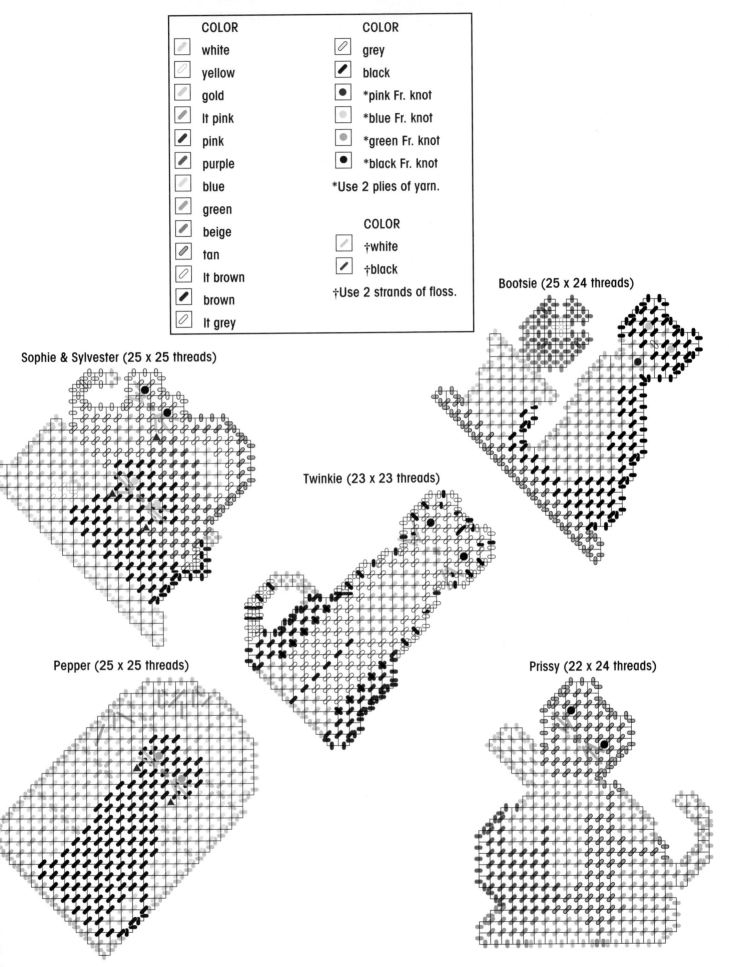

COLOR
- white
- yellow
- gold
- lt pink
- pink
- purple
- blue
- green
- beige
- tan
- lt brown
- brown
- lt grey

COLOR
- grey
- black
- *pink Fr. knot
- *blue Fr. knot
- *green Fr. knot
- *black Fr. knot

*Use 2 plies of yarn.

COLOR
- †white
- †black

†Use 2 strands of floss.

Sophie & Sylvester (25 x 25 threads)

Twinkie (23 x 23 threads)

Bootsie (25 x 24 threads)

Pepper (25 x 25 threads)

Prissy (22 x 24 threads)

Hobby Magnets

Passionate about painting? Crazy about crafts? Or have a quirk for quilting? Then you'll be mad for these magnets inspired by some of our favorite pastimes!

HOBBY MAGNETS

Approx. size: 3"w x 3"h each

Supplies: Worsted weight yarn or Needloft® Plastic Canvas Yarn, Darice® Straw Satin, and black embroidery floss (refer to color key); one 10½" x 13½" sheet of 7 mesh plastic canvas; #16 tapestry needle; magnetic strip; and craft glue.

For Needlepoint: One #24 tapestry needle and red embroidery floss.

For Knitting Basket and Crochet Hook: Metallic silver yarn.

Stitches used: Backstitch, Gobelin Stitch, Mosaic Stitch, Overcast Stitch, Scotch Stitch, and Tent Stitch.

Instructions: Follow charts to cut and stitch desired magnet pieces, working backstitches last.

For Knitting Basket, refer to photo to glue Knitting Needles to back of Knitting Basket.

For Needlepoint, knot a 6" length of red embroidery floss in the eye of #24 tapestry needle. Glue needle under red stitches.

For Paintbrush, refer to photo to wrap and glue 6" of silver yarn around unworked area of canvas.

For Yarn Ball, refer to photo to glue Crochet Hook to Yarn Ball.

Glue magnetic strip to back of magnet.

Designs by Jocelyn Sass.

YARN (NL)	YARN (NL)
white (41)	green (27)
ecru (39)	rust (09)
yellow (57)	brown (13)
orange (11)	metallic silver
pink (07)	
red (02)	**STRAW SATIN (DSS)**
dk red (01)	tan Straw Satin (07)
lt blue (35)	lt brown Straw Satin (09)
blue (32)	
teal (50)	**FLOSS**
lt green (53)	*black
	*Use 6 strands of floss.

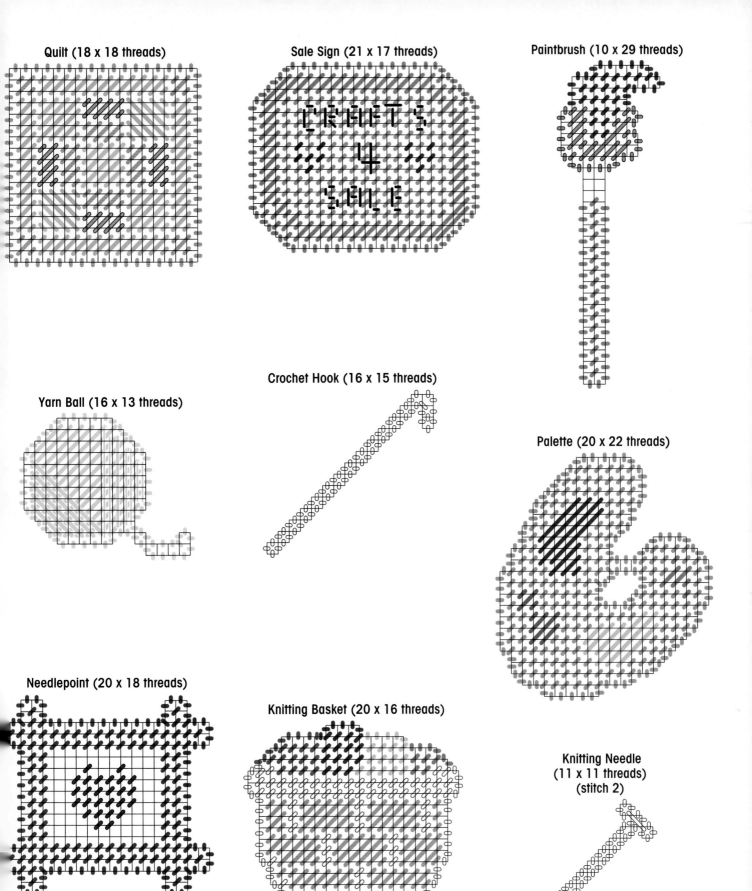

Quilt (18 x 18 threads)

Sale Sign (21 x 17 threads)

Paintbrush (10 x 29 threads)

Crochet Hook (16 x 15 threads)

Yarn Ball (16 x 13 threads)

Palette (20 x 22 threads)

Needlepoint (20 x 18 threads)

Knitting Basket (20 x 16 threads)

Knitting Needle (11 x 11 threads) (stitch 2)

Sunny Sunflowers

These sunflower "patches" will add a splash of color to your message center. The cheery designs can also be glued to wooden dowels for striking plant pokes.

SUNNY SUNFLOWERS

Size: 2¹/₂"w x 2¹/₂"h each

Supplies: Worsted weight yarn or Needloft® Plastic Canvas Yarn (refer to color key), one 10¹/₂" x 13¹/₂" sheet of 7 mesh plastic canvas, #16 tapestry needle, magnetic strip, and craft glue.

Stitches used: Overcast Stitch and Tent Stitch.

Instructions: Follow chart to cut and stitch desired magnet. Glue magnetic strip to back of magnet.

Designs by Polly Carbonari.

COLOR (NL)		COLOR (NL)	
⁄	ecru (39)	⁄	green (27)
⁄	yellow (57)	⁄	brown (13)
⁄	dk yellow (17)	⁄	dk brown (15)
⁄	blue (32)		

Magnet A (17 x 17 threads)

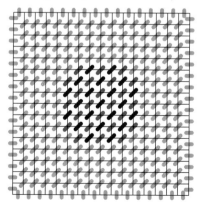

Magnet B (17 x 17 threads)

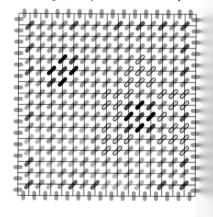

JUST-PICKED MAGNETS

Fruit and veggie lovers will pick this appetizing assortment first! It contains some of their favorite fresh produce — from kiwifruit and pineapple to zucchini squash and cauliflower, plus lots more!

T-PICKED MAGNETS

ox. size: 2¹⁄₂"w x 2¹⁄₂"h each

lies: Darice® Straw Satin (refer to color , one 10¹⁄₂" x 13¹⁄₂" sheet of 7 mesh tic canvas, #16 tapestry needle, netic strip, and craft glue.

Kiwifruit, Orange, or Watermelon: 4¹⁄₄" dia. plastic canvas circle.

Stitches used: Backstitch, Cross Stitch, Gobelin Stitch, Overcast Stitch, Smyrna Cross Stitch, and Tent Stitch.

Instructions: Follow chart to cut and stitch desired magnet, working backstitches last. Referring to photo for color, use overcast stitches to cover unworked edges. Glue magnetic strip to back of magnet.

Designs by Carol Krob.

COLOR (DSS)

- ecru (06)
- yellow (05)
- gold (17)
- orange (20)
- pink (03)
- red (04)
- purple (22)
- dk blue (16)
- lt green (18)
- green (19)
- tan (07)
- lt brown (09)
- brown (11)
- black (12)

Strawberry (15 x 15 threads)

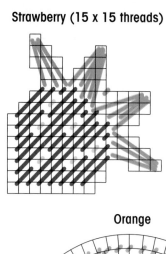

Grapes (20 x 20 threads)

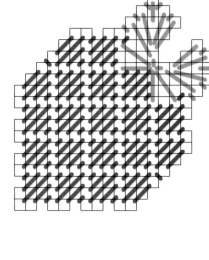

Orange

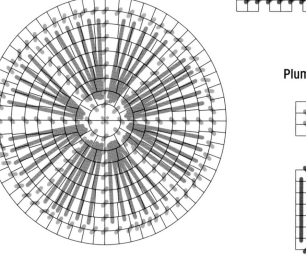

Kiwifruit

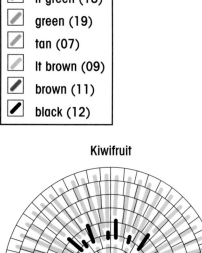

Plum (9 x 17 threads)

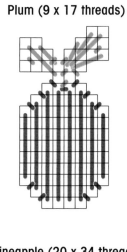

Zucchini Squash (11 x 29 threads)

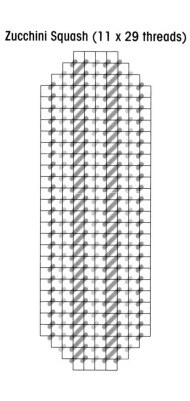

Pineapple (20 x 34 threads)

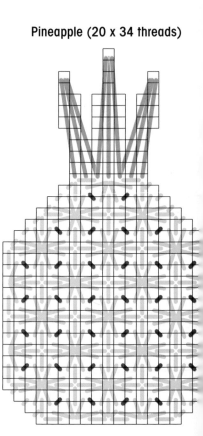

Acorn Squash (21 x 25 threads)

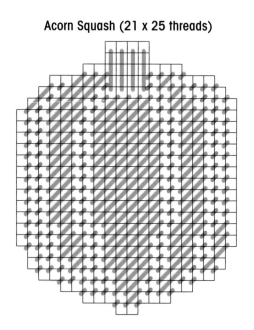

Radish (15 x 24 threads)

Cauliflower (16 x 18 threads)

Broccoli (16 x 25 threads)

Apple (20 x 22 threads)

Pear (17 x 24 threads)

Watermelon

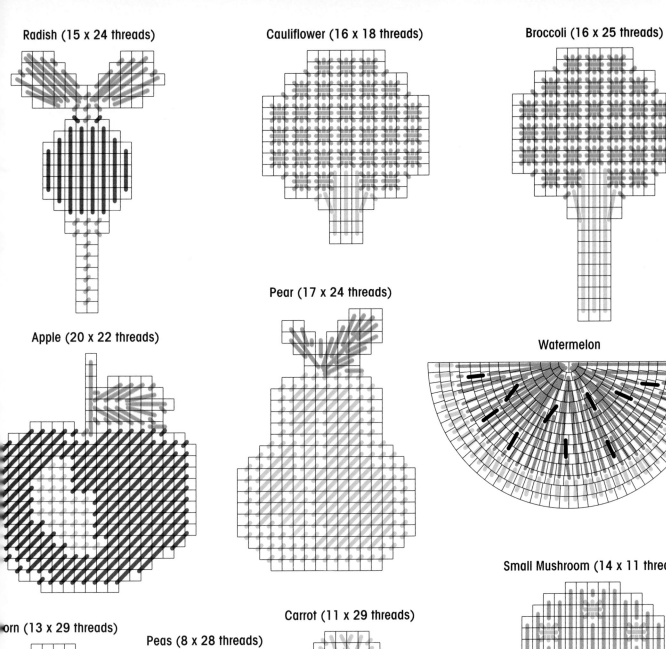

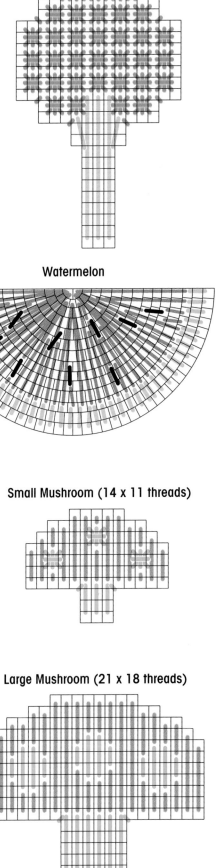

Small Mushroom (14 x 11 threads)

orn (13 x 29 threads)

Peas (8 x 28 threads)

Carrot (11 x 29 threads)

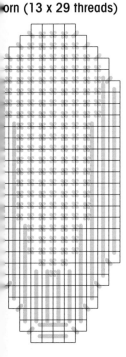

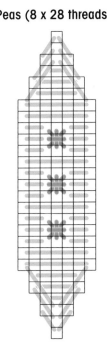

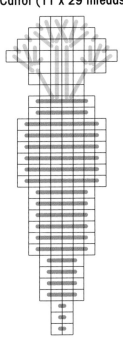

Large Mushroom (21 x 18 threads)

Inspirational Thoughts

These quotations from the Bible are truly inspirational. The three gems are taken from the book of Psalms and make thoughtful little pick-me-up gifts for family and friends.

INSPIRATIONAL THOUGHTS

Size: 2⅝"w x 2½"h each

Supplies: DMC embroidery floss (refer to color key), one 8" x 11" sheet of 14 mesh white plastic canvas, #24 tapestry needle, magnetic strip, and craft glue.

Stitches used: Backstitch, Cross Stitch, French Knot, Gobelin Stitch, Lazy Daisy Stitch, and Tent Stitch.

Instructions: Follow charts to cut and stitch desired magnet, working backstitches and French knots last and using four strands of embroidery floss for the border, th[ ] strands for design area, and two strand[ ] backstitch and Bible verse. Glue magn[ ] strip to back of magnet.

Designs by Ann Townsend.

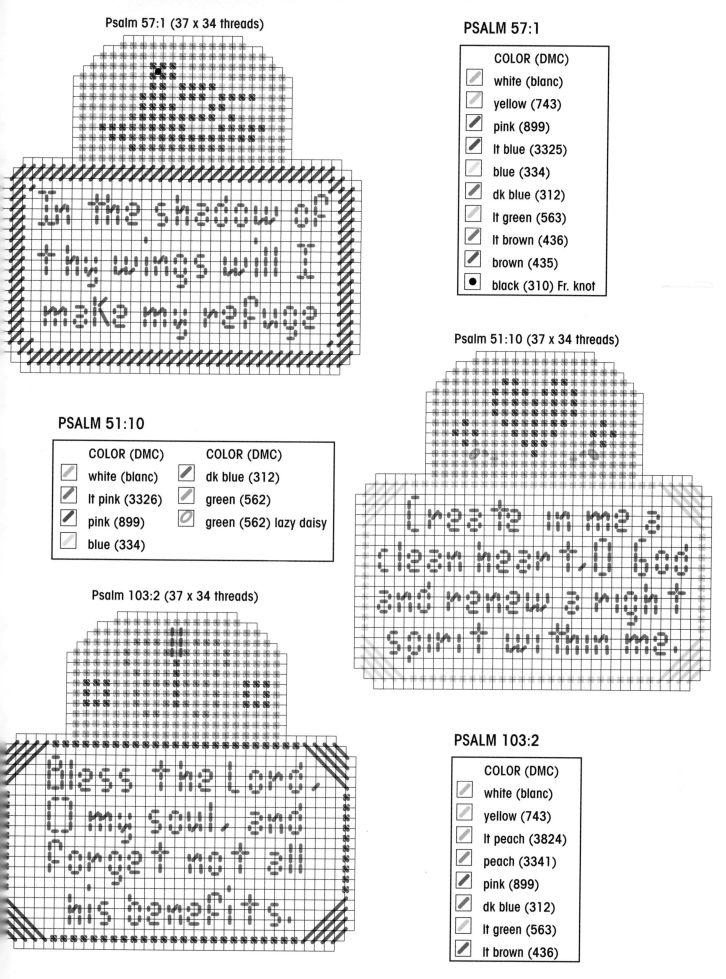

Psalm 57:1 (37 x 34 threads)

In the shadow of thy wings will I make my refuge

PSALM 57:1

	COLOR (DMC)
	white (blanc)
	yellow (743)
	pink (899)
	lt blue (3325)
	blue (334)
	dk blue (312)
	lt green (563)
	lt brown (436)
	brown (435)
●	black (310) Fr. knot

PSALM 51:10

	COLOR (DMC)		COLOR (DMC)
	white (blanc)		dk blue (312)
	lt pink (3326)		green (562)
	pink (899)		green (562) lazy daisy
	blue (334)		

Psalm 51:10 (37 x 34 threads)

Create in me a clean heart, O God and renew a right spirit within me.

Psalm 103:2 (37 x 34 threads)

Bless the Lord, O my soul, and forget not all his benefits.

PSALM 103:2

	COLOR (DMC)
	white (blanc)
	yellow (743)
	lt peach (3824)
	peach (3341)
	pink (899)
	dk blue (312)
	lt green (563)
	lt brown (436)

Country Life

*This cute collection captures all the things we love best about country
living — farm-fresh eggs, red delicious apples, juicy strawberries, and more.*

COUNTRY LIFE

Approx. size: 3"w x 3"h each

Supplies: Worsted weight yarn and embroidery floss (refer to color key), one 10½" x 13½" sheet of 7 mesh plastic canvas, #16 tapestry needle, #24 tapestry needle, magnetic strip, and craft glue.

Stitches used: Backstitch, French Knot, Overcast Stitch, and Tent Stitch.

Instructions: Follow chart to cut and stitch desired magnet, working backstitches and French knots last. Glue magnetic strip to back of magnet.

For Love Jar, tie an 8" length of lt blue yarn in a bow; trim ends. Referring to photo, glue bow to Love Jar.

Designs by Lorraine Birmingham.

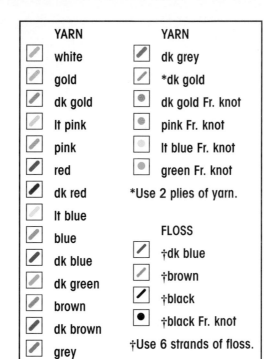

YARN		YARN	
⬜	white	⬜	dk grey
⬜	gold	⬜	*dk gold
⬜	dk gold	⬤	dk gold Fr. knot
⬜	lt pink	⬤	pink Fr. knot
⬜	pink	⬤	lt blue Fr. knot
⬜	red	⬤	green Fr. knot
⬜	dk red	*Use 2 plies of yarn.	
⬜	lt blue		
⬜	blue	FLOSS	
⬜	dk blue	⬜	†dk blue
⬜	dk green	⬜	†brown
⬜	brown	⬜	†black
⬜	dk brown	⬤	†black Fr. knot
⬜	grey	†Use 6 strands of floss.	

Apple Bowl (20 x 18 threads)

Crock of Pears (19 x 23 threads)

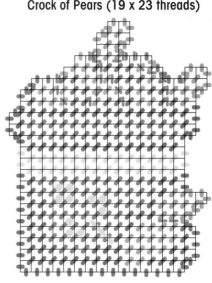

Love Jar (19 x 19 threads)

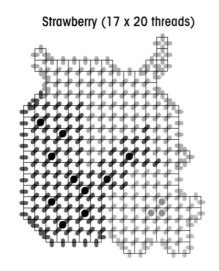

Strawberry (17 x 20 threads)

Teapot (22 x 23 threads)

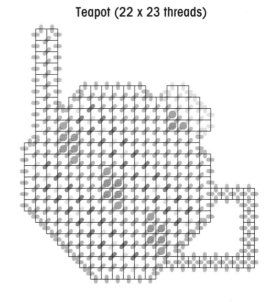

Egg Crate (23 x 17 threads)

Pleasing Patchwork

Inspired by popular quilt blocks, these patchwork magnets capture the charm of handmade quilts — especially when they're displayed in a decorative grouping!

PLEASING PATCHWORK

Size: 1³/₈"w x 1³/₈"h each

Supplies: Embroidery floss (refer to photo), one 10¹/₂" x 13¹/₂" sheet of 10 mesh plastic canvas, #20 tapestry needle, magnetic strip, and craft glue.

Stitches used: Gobelin Stitch, Overcast Stitch, Scotch Stitch, and Tent Stitch.

Instructions: The photography models were stitched with DMC 336, 640, 816, and 822. Follow chart to cut and stitch desired magnet, using 12 strands of embroidery floss for all stitches. Use overcast stitches to cover unworked edges. Glue magnetic strip to back of magnet.

Designs by Mary Billeaudeau.

COLOR	
✎	color A
✎	color B
✎	color C
✎	color D

Quilt #1 (14 x 14 threads)

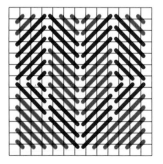

Quilt #2 (14 x 14 threads)

Quilt #3 (14 x 14 threads)

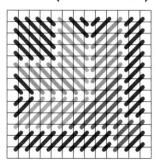

Quilt #4 (14 x 14 threads)

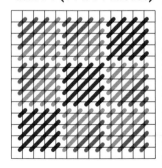

Flowers and Romance

You can re-create the soft beauty of a flower bed with these floral motifs. The twenty designs are fashioned in pleasing pastels for a touch of romance.

Reminder:
- Flowers for Shower
- Silk Ribbon
- Wrapping Paper

To Do:
- Pick Up Top Soil
- Hostas
- Tea Roses

(17 x 17 threads)

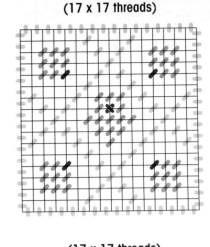

(17 x 17 threads)

(17 x 17 threads)

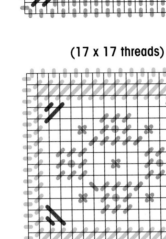

(17 x 17 threads)

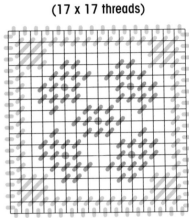

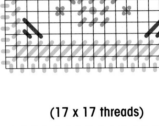

	COLOR (NL)
/	white (41)
/	yellow (20)
/	pink (07)
/	dk pink (05)
/	lt purple (45)
/	purple (46)
/	blue (35)
/	dk blue (48)
/	green (53)
•	yellow (20) Fr. knot

(17 x 17 threads)

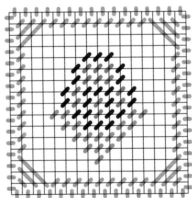

(17 x 17 threads)

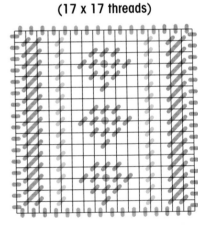
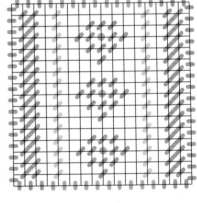

FLOWERS AND ROMANCE

Approx. size: 2½"w x 2½"h each
Supplies: Worsted weight yarn or Needloft® Plastic Canvas Yarn (refer to color key), one 10½" x 13½" sheet of 7 mesh plastic canvas, #16 tapestry needle, magnetic strip, and craft glue.
Stitches used: Backstitch, Cross Stitch, Double French Knot, Gobelin Stitch, Mosaic Stitch, Overcast Stitch, Scotch Stitch, and Tent Stitch.
Instructions: Follow chart to cut and stitch desired magnet, completing background with white tent stitches before adding backstitches and double French knots. Glue magnetic strip to back of magnet.

Designs by Ann Townsend.

(17 x 17 threads)

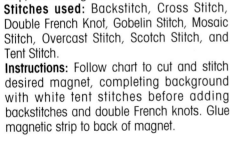

(17 x 17 threads)

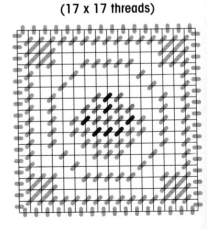

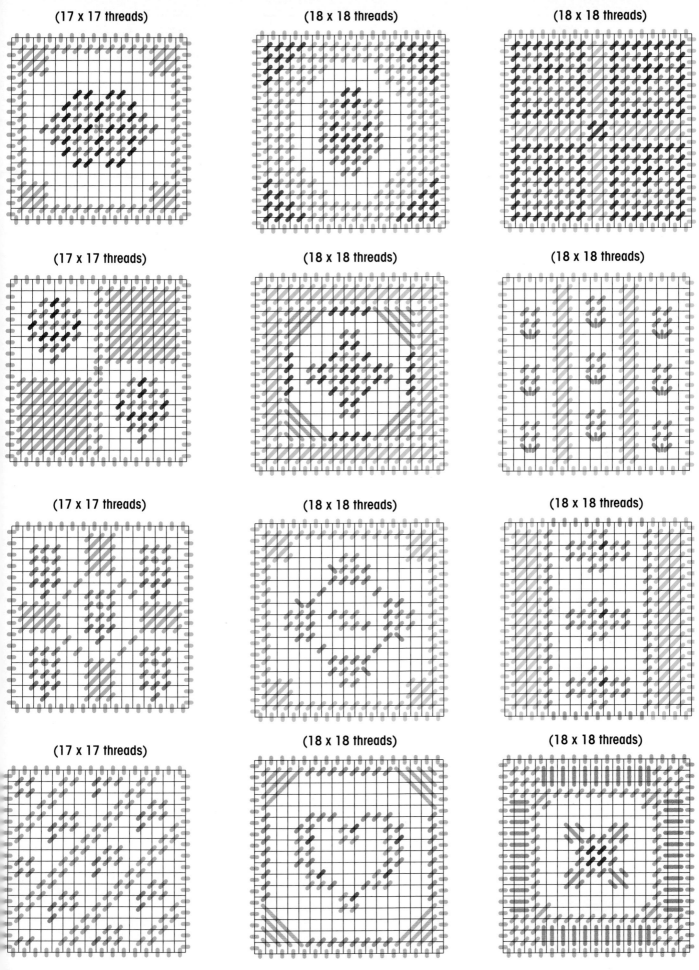

(17 x 17 threads)   (18 x 18 threads)   (18 x 18 threads)

(17 x 17 threads)   (18 x 18 threads)   (18 x 18 threads)

(17 x 17 threads)   (18 x 18 threads)   (18 x 18 threads)

(17 x 17 threads)   (18 x 18 threads)   (18 x 18 threads)

65

Bears, Bears, Bears!

Teddy bear collectors will find this medley of magnets tempting!
One basic pattern is combined with dozens of motifs
for all occasions to create the "beary" cute set.

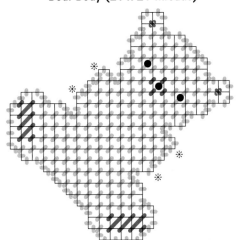

Bear Body (21 x 21 threads)

Bear Paw
(6 x 6 threads) (stitch 2)

EARS, BEARS, BEARS

prox. size: 2¹/₂"w x 3"h each

pplies: Worsted weight yarn (refer to or keys), one 10¹/₂" x 13¹/₂" sheet of mesh clear plastic canvas, #16 tapestry edle, magnetic strip, and craft glue.

r Baby Bear: One 10¹/₂" x 13¹/₂" sheet of mesh white plastic canvas and one 2¹/₂" gth of 3mm white chenille stem.

r Balloon Bear: One 2" length of 3mm ite chenille stem.

r Boating Bear: One 1¹/₂" length of 3mm ite chenille stem.

r Bear with Fishing Pole: One 3¹/₂" gth of 3mm brown chenille stem.

r Bear with Flower Basket: One ¹/₂" x 13¹/₂" sheet of 7 mesh white stic canvas, one 3" length of 3mm white nille stem, and small artificial flowers.

Bear with Umbrella: One 2" length of m white chenille stem.

Graduate Bear: 1¹/₂" square of white er and 12" length of metallic gold ad.

I ❤ Dad Bear: One 10¹/₂" x 13¹/₂" et of 7 mesh lt blue plastic canvas.

I ❤ Mom Bear: One 10¹/₂" x 13¹/₂" et of 7 mesh pink plastic canvas.

Party Bear: Kreinik ¹/₈"w metallic gold on.

ches used: Backstitch, Cross Stitch, ch Knot, Gobelin Stitch, Overcast Stitch, ersed Tent Stitch, and Tent Stitch.

Instructions: *Use matching color overcast stitches when joining unless otherwise noted.* Follow charts to cut and stitch Bear and Bear Paws, working French knots last. With wrong side of Paws on right side of Bear, match ✳'s and use matching color yarn to join Paws to Bear. Follow charts to cut and stitch desired decorations, working backstitches and French knots last. Assemble decorations as follows:

For Baby Bear: Glue chenille stem to Baby Basket at ★'s.

For Balloon Bear: Refer to photo to glue chenille stem to back of Balloon.

For Boating Bear: Refer to photo to glue chenille stem to back of Sail and Boat.

For Bear with Book: Matching ▲'s, join Book Front and Book Back to Book Spine.

For Bear with Fishing Pole: Refer to photo and make two loops in chenille stem to form pole. Thread a 12" length of white 2-ply yarn through loops on pole. Trim ends of yarn and glue ends and pole to wrong side of one Paw. Thread a 12" length of black 2-ply yarn through each Fish; secure. Trim loose end of yarn to 1" and glue to wrong side of other Paw.

For Bear with Flower Basket: Matching ◆'s, fold Flower Basket in half. Use white overcast stitches to join edges. Refer to photo to glue chenille stem between Flower Basket halves. Glue flowers in Flower Basket.

For Bear with Kite: Refer to photo to tie a 10" length of black 2-ply yarn around Bows; trim end. Secure to back of Kite.

For Bear with Present: Tie a 10" length of red yarn in a bow; trim ends. Refer to photo to glue bow to Present.

For Bear with Umbrella: Refer to photo to glue chenille stem to back of Umbrella.

For Bear with Wreath: Tie a 10" length of red yarn in a bow; trim ends. Refer to photo to glue bow to Wreath.

For Graduate Bear: Join short ends of Brim. Cut an 8" length of white yarn. Tie a knot close to one end. Refer to photo to attach yarn to center of Cap; trim ends. For tassel, separate yarn below knot. Glue Brim to center of Cap. For diploma, roll 1¹/₂" square of white paper and tie with metallic gold thread.

For I ❤ Dad and I ❤ Mom Bears: Cut paper same size as Frame Back. Write message on paper. Glue paper between Front and Back.

For Indian Bear: Join short ends of Headband. Refer to photo to glue Feathers to Headband.

For Party Bear: Matching ◆'s, join straight edges of Party Hat, forming a cone shape.

Refer to photo to glue decorations to Bear. Glue magnetic strip to back of Bear.

Designs by Melanna Rosenthal and Joan Bartling.

Party Hat (10 x 10 threads)

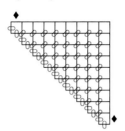

Glass (4 x 7 threads)

Bottle (8 x 8 threads)

Present (8 x 11 threads)

Balloon (8 x 8 threads)

Umbrella (10 x 10 threads)

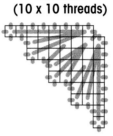

Sail (5 x 4 threads)

Boat (9 x 5 threads)

Heart (10 x 9 threads)

Egg (10 x 10 threads)

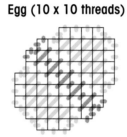

Fish (6 x 6 threads) (stitch 2)

Shamrock (10 x 10 threads)

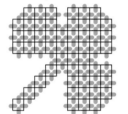

Flower Basket (14 x 14 threads) Cut from white canvas.

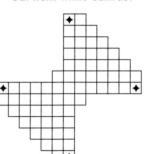

Rattle (8 x 8 threads) Cut from white canvas.

Baby Basket (8 x 8 threads) Cut from white canvas.

Bow (3 x 3 threads) (stitch 2)

Kite (13 x 10 threads)

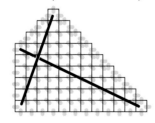

Frame Front (10 x 10 threads) Cut from pink or lt blue canvas.

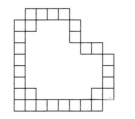

Frame Back (10 x 10 threads) Cut from pink or lt blue canvas.

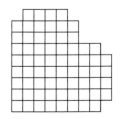

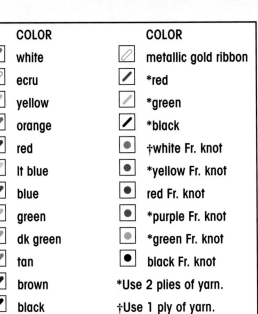

COLOR		COLOR	
	white		metallic gold ribbon
	ecru		*red
	yellow		*green
	orange		*black
	red	●	†white Fr. knot
	lt blue	●	*yellow Fr. knot
	blue	●	red Fr. knot
	green	●	*purple Fr. knot
	dk green	●	*green Fr. knot
	tan	●	black Fr. knot
	brown		*Use 2 plies of yarn.
	black		†Use 1 ply of yarn.

Red Feather
(5 x 5 threads)

Orange Feather
(5 x 5 threads)

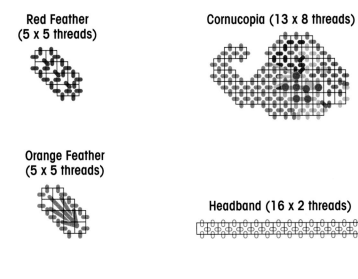

Cornucopia (13 x 8 threads)

Headband (16 x 2 threads)

Corn
(5 x 5 threads)

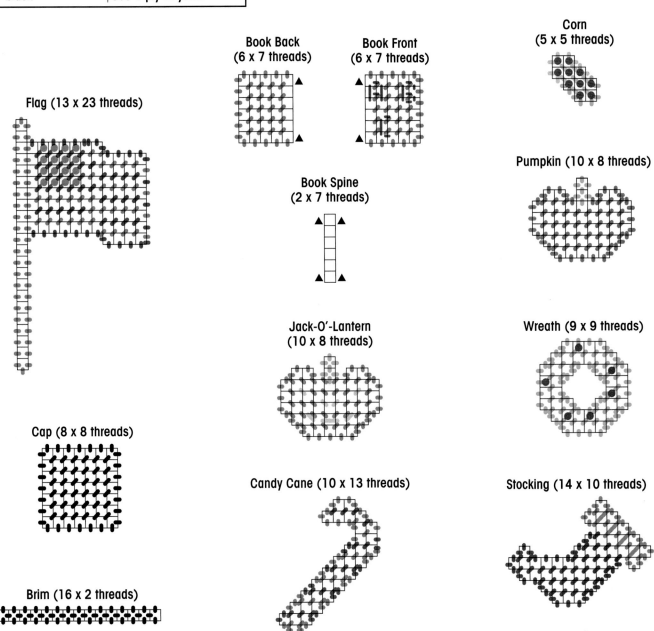

Flag (13 x 23 threads)

Book Back
(6 x 7 threads)

Book Front
(6 x 7 threads)

Book Spine
(2 x 7 threads)

Pumpkin (10 x 8 threads)

Jack-O'-Lantern
(10 x 8 threads)

Wreath (9 x 9 threads)

Cap (8 x 8 threads)

Candy Cane (10 x 13 threads)

Stocking (14 x 10 threads)

Brim (16 x 2 threads)

69

Licensed to Celebrate

These clever magnets are your license to celebrate! Stitched with fun messages, the mini plates will make festive decorations for holidays throughout the year.

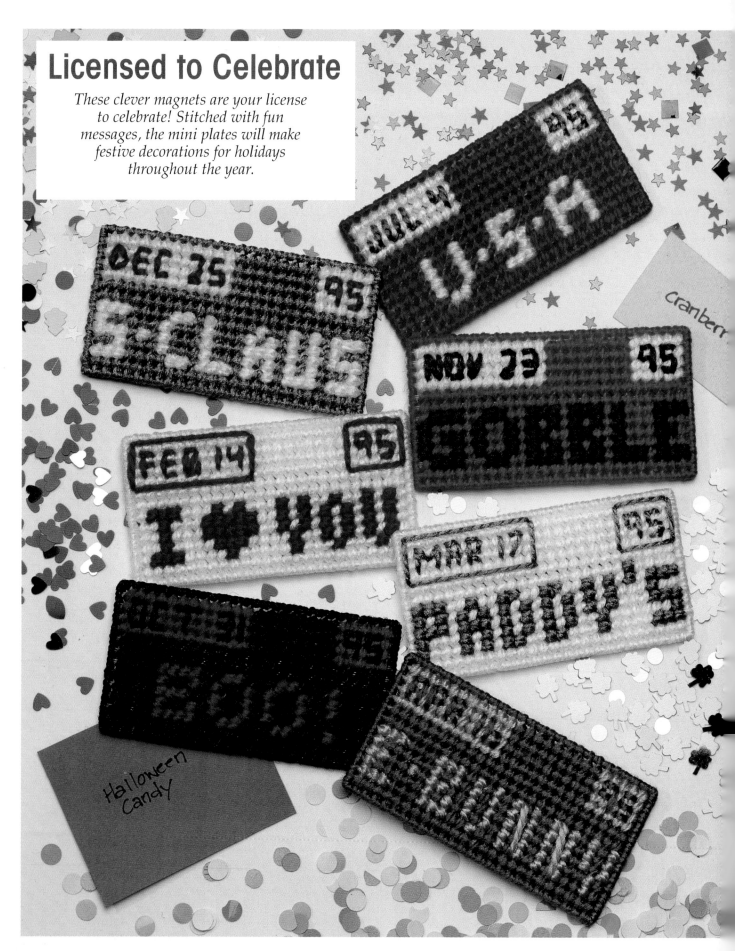

CENSED TO CELEBRATE

Size: 4"w x 2"h each

Supplies: Worsted weight yarn or Needloft®
Plastic Canvas Yarn (refer to color key),
one 10¹/₂" x 13¹/₂" sheet of 7 mesh plastic
canvas, #16 tapestry needle, magnetic
strip, and craft glue.

Stitches used: Backstitch, Cross Stitch,
Overcast Stitch, and Tent Stitch.

Instructions: Follow chart to cut and stitch
desired magnet, completing background as
indicated on chart before adding
backstitches. Change dates using additional
numbers provided. Glue magnetic strip to
back of magnet.

Designs by Diane W. Villano.

COLOR (NL)		COLOR (NL)	
	white (41)		purple (46)
	yellow (57)		blue (32)
	orange (52)		green (27)
	pink (07)		brown (15)
	red (02)		black (00)

Numbers

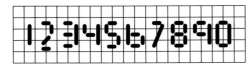

February (27 x 14 threads)

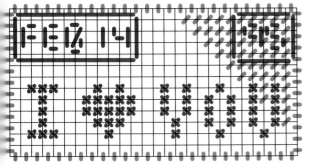

March (27 x 14 threads)

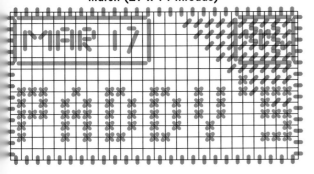

April (27 x 14 threads)

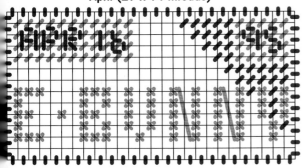

July (27 x 14 threads)

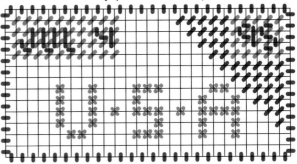

October (27 x 14 threads)

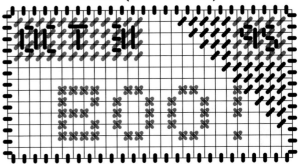

November (27 x 14 threads)

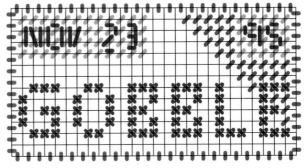

December (27 x 14 threads)

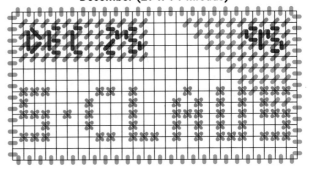

71

HOLIDAY HOLD-UPS

You'll want to put these holiday hold-ups at the top of your project list! The cheery little magnets not only make sweet gifts, but they also offer a great way to humor yourself by adding seasonal fun to your message center.

HOLIDAY HOLD-UPS

Approx. size: 3¹/₄"w x 3¹/₄"h each

Supplies: Worsted weight yarn or Needloft®
Plastic Canvas Yarn (refer to color keys),
one 10¹/₂" x 13¹/₂" sheet of 7 mesh plastic
canvas, #16 tapestry needle, magnetic
strip, and craft glue.

For Turkey: Two 4" lengths of 3mm black
chenille stem.

Stitches used: Backstitch, French Knot,
Fringe Stitch, Overcast Stitch, and Tent
Stitch.

Instructions: Follow chart(s) to cut and
stitch desired magnet piece(s), working
backstitches, French knots, and fringe
stitches last. Refer to photo to glue pieces
together. Glue magnetic strip to back of
magnet.

For Turkey: For legs and feet, refer to photo
and insert a chenille stem into each thigh.
Twist ends together, bending ends in
opposite directions for feet.

Designs by Maryanne Moreck.

	COLOR (NL)		COLOR (NL)
	white (41)		lt blue (35)
	yellow (19)		dk blue (48)
	orange (52)		lt green (53)
	flesh (56)		green (27)
	lt pink (07)		beige (40)
	pink (55)		dk tan (13)
	red (01)		black (00)
	lt purple (45)	●	black (00) Fr. knot
	purple (46)		

Valentine Bouquet (28 x 23 threads)

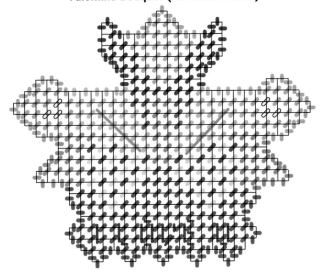

Easter Basket (25 x 24 threads)

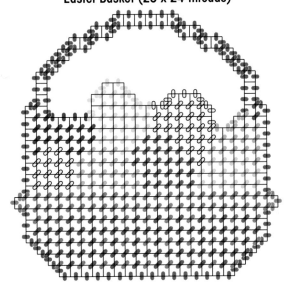

Easter Basket Bow (13 x 6 threads)

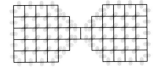

Chick (20 x 22 threads)

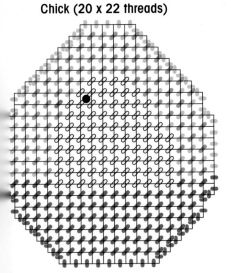

Eggshell (20 x 11 threads)

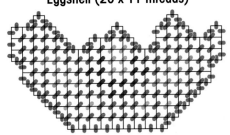

Uncle Sam (18 x 26 threads)

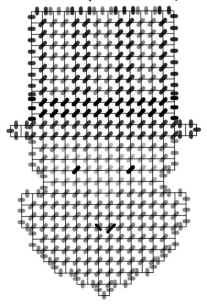

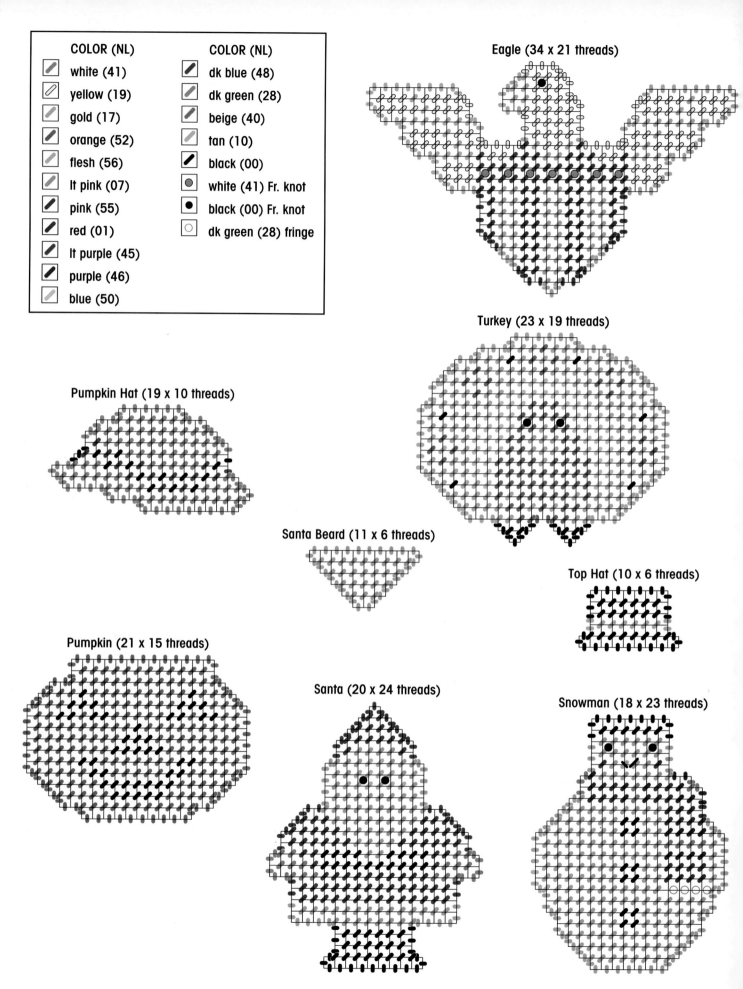

COLOR (NL)

white (41)	
yellow (19)	
gold (17)	
orange (52)	
flesh (56)	
lt pink (07)	
pink (55)	
red (01)	
lt purple (45)	
purple (46)	
blue (50)	

COLOR (NL)

dk blue (48)	
dk green (28)	
beige (40)	
tan (10)	
black (00)	
white (41) Fr. knot	
black (00) Fr. knot	
dk green (28) fringe	

Eagle (34 x 21 threads)

Turkey (23 x 19 threads)

Pumpkin Hat (19 x 10 threads)

Santa Beard (11 x 6 threads)

Top Hat (10 x 6 threads)

Pumpkin (21 x 15 threads)

Santa (20 x 24 threads)

Snowman (18 x 23 threads)

Merry Magnets

These merry magnets bring festive fun to holidays throughout the year. You can transform them into lapel pins by simply gluing pin backs to the designs.

MERRY MAGNETS

Approx. size: 3"w x 3"h each

Supplies: Worsted weight yarn and Kreinik ⅛" metallic gold ribbon (refer to color key), one 10½" x 13½" sheet of 7 mesh plastic canvas, #16 tapestry needle, magnetic strip, and craft glue.

Stitches used: Backstitch, French Knot, Gobelin Stitch, Overcast Stitch, Tent Stitch, and Upright Cross Stitch.

Instructions: Follow chart(s) to cut and stitch desired magnet piece(s), working backstitches and French knots last. Glue magnetic strip to back of magnet.

For Angel: Matching ▲'s and ★'s, use white to join Angel Arms to Angel. Tie a 10" length of red yarn in a bow; trim ends. Refer to photo to glue bow to Wreath.

For Basket: Tie a 10" length of pink yarn in a bow; trim ends. Refer to photo to glue bow to Basket.

For Bunny: Matching ▲'s and ★'s, use lt tan to join Bunny Arms to Bunny. Tie a 10" length of lavender yarn in a bow; trim ends. Refer to photo to glue bow to Bunny.

For Chick: Tie a 10" length of lavender yarn in a bow; trim ends. Refer to photo to glue bow to Chick.

For Witch: Tie a 10" length of orange yarn in a bow; trim ends. Refer to photo to glue bow to Witch.

For Cupid: Matching ▲'s and ★'s, use flesh to tack Cupid Arm to Cupid.

Designs by Dick Martin.

Cupid Arm (6 x 5 threads)

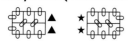

Cupid (16 x 17 threads)

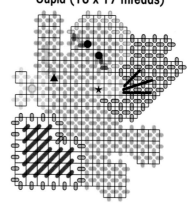

Heart (16 x 16 threads)

Rainbow (16 x 16 threads)

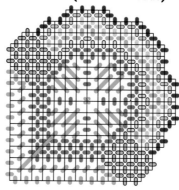

Leprechaun (22 x 22 threads)

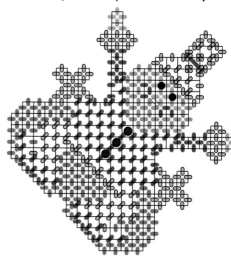

Chick (17 x 17 threads)

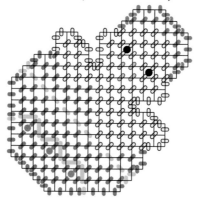

Angel Arms (9 x 9 threads)

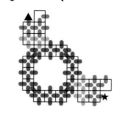

Bunny Arms (4 x 3 threads)

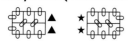

Bunny (20 x 20 threads)

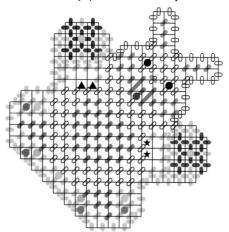

Basket (18 x 18 threads)

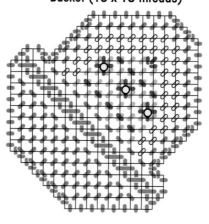

Angel (18 x 18 threads)

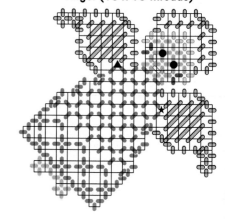

COLOR	COLOR	COLOR
white	dk blue	○ lt yellow Fr. knot
lt yellow	navy	yellow Fr. knot
yellow	aqua	lt gold Fr. knot
lt gold	vy lt green	● *orange Fr. knot
lt orange	lt green	● lt pink Fr. knot
orange	green	pink Fr. knot
flesh	dk green	● red Fr. knot
lt pink	rust	● lavender Fr. knot
pink	lt tan	purple Fr. knot
red	dk tan	lt blue Fr. knot
lavender	brown	◎ lt green Fr. knot
purple	black	● *black Fr. knot
lt blue	metallic gold	● metallic gold Fr. knot
blue	*black	*Use 2 plies of yarn.

Eagle (17 x 17 threads)

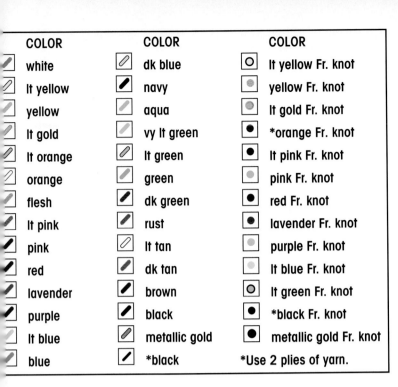

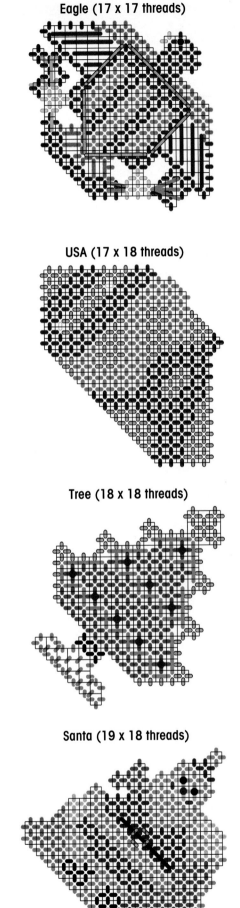

USA (17 x 18 threads)

Witch (18 x 19 threads)

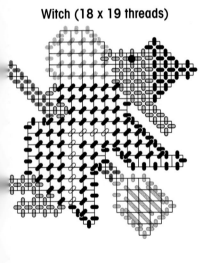

Pumpkin (21 x 21 threads)

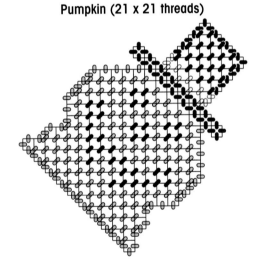

Tree (18 x 18 threads)

Reindeer (16 x 19 threads)

Cat (19 x 19 threads)

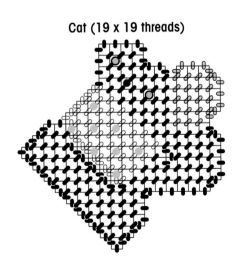

Santa (19 x 18 threads)

HOLIDAY TRIO

These charming magnets will help you celebrate St. Patrick's Day, Valentine's Day, and Washington's Birthday in style!

HOLIDAY TRIO

Approx. size: 4"w x 3¹/₂"h each
Supplies: Worsted weight yarn or Needloft® Plastic Canvas Yarn (refer to color key), one 10¹/₂" x 13¹/₂" sheet of 7 mesh plastic canvas, #16 tapestry needle, magnetic strip, and craft glue.
For Valentine's Day Magnet: Metallic gold yarn.
For Washington's Birthday Magnet: One 6" length of green cloth-covered wire, two 5" lengths of green cloth-covered wire, and green floral tape.
For St. Patrick's Day Magnet: Metallic gold yarn and one 3" dia. plastic canvas circle.
Stitches used: Backstitch, Double French Knot, Overcast Stitch, and Tent Stitch.

Instructions:
For Valentine's Day Magnet, follow charts to cut and stitch "I Love You" Sign, Heart Front, and Heart Back, working backstitches last. Using metallic gold yarn, join Heart Front to Heart Back along unworked edges. Referring to photo, glue Heart to Sign. Glue magnetic strip to back of magnet.
For Washington's Birthday Magnet, follow charts to cut and stitch Ax and Cherries. Thread one length of wire through each Cherry. Fold wire in half and wrap with floral tape. Hold ends of all three wire lengths together and wrap with floral tape for 1¹/₂". Tie a 6" length of green yarn in a bow around wires; trim ends. Referring to photo, glue Cherries and stem to Ax. Glue magnetic strip to back of magnet.

For St. Patrick's Day Magnet, follo charts to cut and stitch Shamrock, Pot, ar Rainbow, working double French knots las Glue Pot and Rainbow to Shamroc Referring to photo, work metallic go double French knots on Pot and Rainbo Glue magnetic strip to back of magnet.

Valentine's Day Magnet design l Jessi-ann Maieli.
Washington's Birthday Magnet design Lennia Mertz.
St. Patrick's Day Magnet design by Cati Eisenhauer.

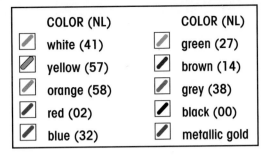

COLOR (NL)		COLOR (NL)	
white (41)		green (27)	
yellow (57)		brown (14)	
orange (58)		grey (38)	
red (02)		black (00)	
blue (32)		metallic gold	

"I Love You" Sign (22 x 22 threads)

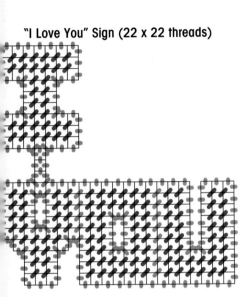

Ax (32 x 16 threads)

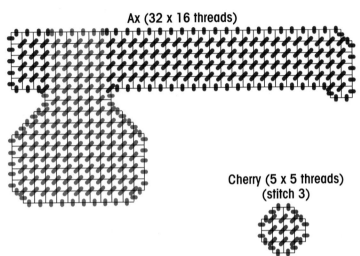

Cherry (5 x 5 threads)
(stitch 3)

Shamrock (25 x 24 threads)

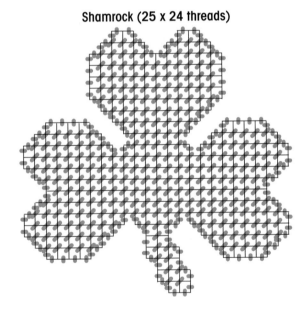

Heart Front (12 x 12 threads)

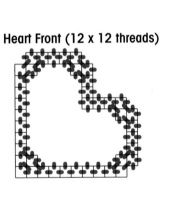

Heart Back (12 x 12 threads)

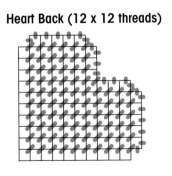

Pot (11 x 7 threads)

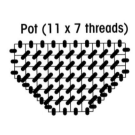

Rainbow
Cut from plastic canvas circle.

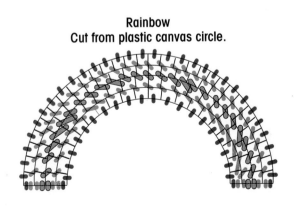

Itsy-Bitsy Bunny Baskets

Brimming with springtime cheer, these little baskets are just the right size for our easy-to-make pom-pom bunnies. The versatile designs can be finished as magnets or as pins to wear on Easter.

Y-BITSY BUNNY BASKETS

Size: 1"w x 2¼"h x 1"d each

Supplies: Sport weight yarn (refer to color key), one 10½" x 13½" sheet of 10 mesh plastic canvas, #20 tapestry needle, two ½" white pom-poms, five 5mm white pom-poms, two 3mm moving eyes, one pink seed bead, two 1½" lengths of 6mm white chenille stem, magnetic strip, and craft glue.

Stitches used: Overcast Stitch and Reversed Slant Stitch.

Instructions: Follow charts to cut and stitch desired magnet pieces. Matching ▲'s and ★'s, use white overcast stitches to join Basket to Back. Refer to photo to tack Handle to Back. Refer to Diagram to assemble bunny. For head and body, glue ½" pom-poms together. For paws, glue four 5mm pom-poms to body. For tail, glue remaining pom-pom to back of body. For ears, bend chenille stems in half and glue ends to back of head. Glue eyes to head. For nose, glue seed bead to head. For bow, tie a 6" length of yarn in a bow; trim ends. Glue bow to bunny. Glue bunny in Basket. Glue magnetic strip to Back.

Designs by Eleanor Albano.

Diagram

COLOR		COLOR	
▨ white		▨ lavender	
▨ yellow		▨ blue	
▨ pink		▨ green	

Basket #1 (22 x 9 threads)

Basket #3 (22 x 9 threads)

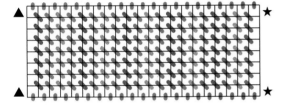

Basket #5 (22 x 9 threads)

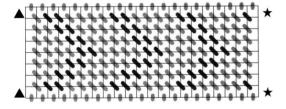

Basket #2 (22 x 9 threads)

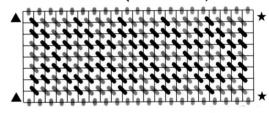

Basket #4 (22 x 9 threads)

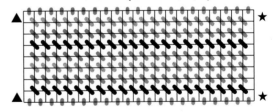

Back (9 x 9 threads)

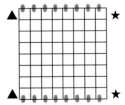

Handle (30 x 3 threads)

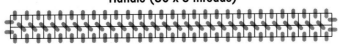

81

Haunting Magnets

These fun spooks have a certain "magnetic" charm! They'll make great party decorations or cute touches to add to bags of Halloween candy.

AUNTING MAGNETS

Size: 4"w x 4½"h each

Supplies: Worsted weight yarn (refer to color key), one 10½" x 13½" sheet of mesh plastic canvas, #16 tapestry needle, magnetic strip, and craft glue.
For Witch: Fine-tooth comb.

Stitches used: Backstitch, Lazy Daisy Stitch, Overcast Stitch, Tent Stitch, and Turkey Loop.

Instructions:

For Witch, follow chart to cut and stitch Witch, working backstitches and 4" long Turkey loops last. Referring to photo for yarn color, cover unworked edges. Clip Turkey loops and separate each strand into plies. Comb each strand until the desired look is achieved. Refer to photo and trim ends to 2". Glue magnetic strip to back of magnet.

For Cat and Moon, follow charts to cut and stitch Cat and Moon pieces, working backstitches and lazy daisy stitches last. Referring to photo for yarn color, cover unworked edges. Glue Cat to Moon. Glue magnetic strip to back of magnet.
For all others, follow chart to cut and stitch desired magnet, working backstitches and lazy daisy stitches last. Referring to photo for yarn color, cover unworked edges. Glue magnetic strip to back of magnet.

Witch design by Jamie Sue Taubenheim.
Cat and Moon design by Clara M. Albert.
Boo design by Virginia Hockenbury.
Pumpkin design by Laurie Monahan.

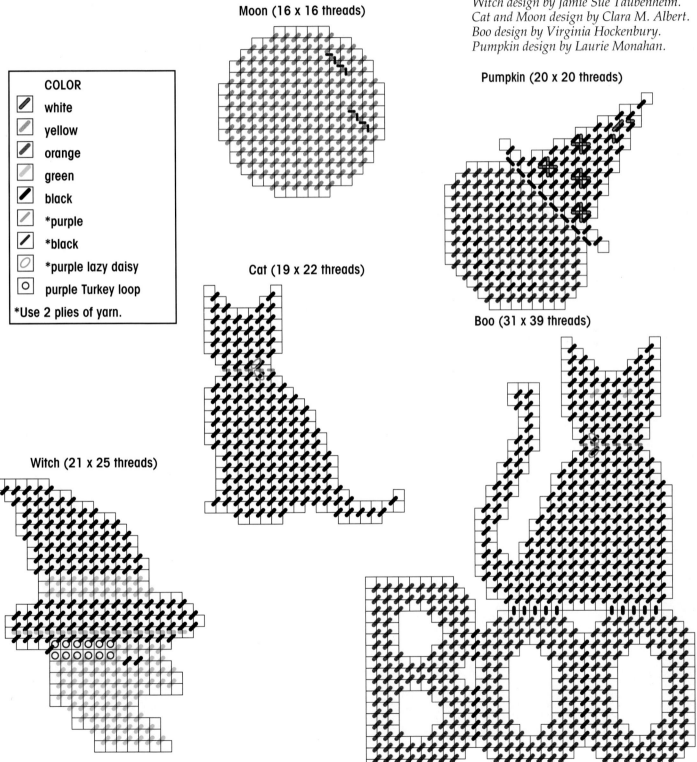

COLOR

⟋	white
⟋	yellow
⟋	orange
⟋	green
⟋	black
⟋	*purple
⟋	*black
⊘	*purple lazy daisy
⊙	purple Turkey loop

*Use 2 plies of yarn.

Moon (16 x 16 threads)

Pumpkin (20 x 20 threads)

Cat (19 x 22 threads)

Boo (31 x 39 threads)

Witch (21 x 25 threads)

Glow-in-the-Dark Ghouls

Stitched with glow-in-the-dark braid, these six spooky magnets will make your Halloween positively "illuminating!"

LOW-IN-THE-DARK GHOULS

prox. size: 2¹/₂"w x 2¹/₂"h each

pplies: Kreinik #32 heavy braid and black embroidery floss (refer to lor key), one 10¹/₂" x 13¹/₂" sheet of 10 mesh plastic canvas, '0 tapestry needle, magnetic strip, and craft glue.

tches used: Backstitch, Cross Stitch, French Knot, Gobelin Stitch, ercast Stitch, and Tent Stitch.

structions: Follow chart to cut and stitch desired magnet, working ckstitches and French knots last. Glue magnetic strip to back of magnet.

signs by Joan Green.

Bat (31 x 15 threads)

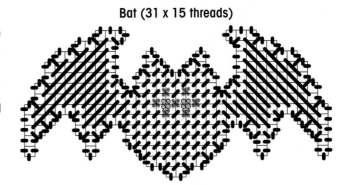

COLOR (KREINIK)	
⬁	ivory (052F)
⬁	yellow (054F)
⬁	orange (051F)
⬁	pink (055F)
⬁	green (053F)
⬤	green (053F) Fr. knot

COLOR (FLOSS)	
⬁	*black
⬁	†black
⬤	*black Fr. Knot

*Use 12 strands of embroidery floss.

†Use 6 strands of embroidery floss.

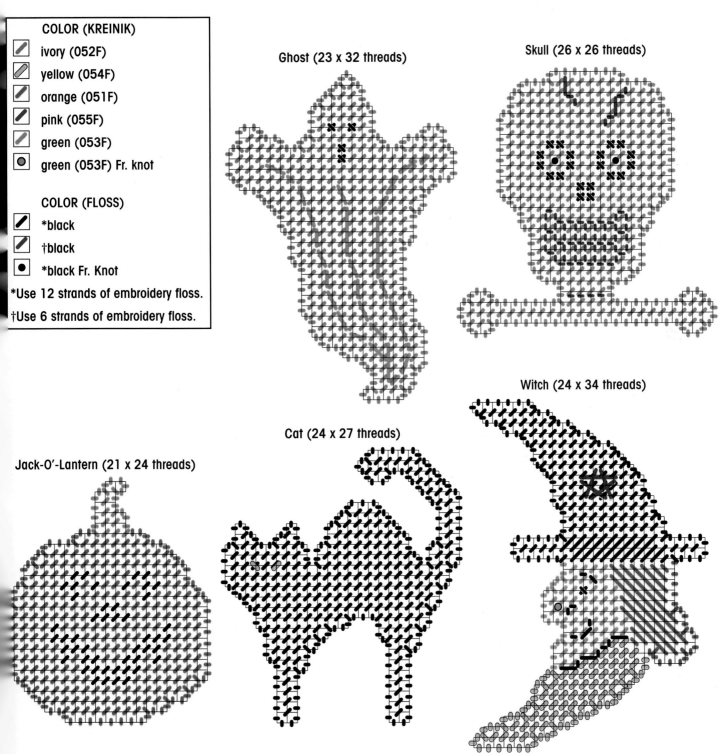

Ghost (23 x 32 threads)

Skull (26 x 26 threads)

Witch (24 x 34 threads)

Cat (24 x 27 threads)

Jack-O'-Lantern (21 x 24 threads)

Dazzling Fall Leaves

Every fall, Mother Nature paints her canvas of leafy trees in rich hues of gold, red, and orange. We captured the wonder of that transformation with these colorful magnets. They're a vibrant way to post your autumn-time reminders!

AZZLING FALL LEAVES

prox. size: 3"w x 4¹/₂"h each

pplies: Worsted weight yarn and metallic
rn (refer to photo), one 10¹/₂" x 13¹/₂"
eet of 7 mesh plastic canvas,
6 tapestry needle, magnetic strip, and
aft glue.

itches used: Backstitch, Overcast Stitch,
d Tent Stitch.

structions: Follow chart to cut and stitch
sired magnet, working backstitches last.
ing metallic color overcast stitches, cover
worked edges of magnet. Glue magnetic
ip to back of magnet.

esigns by Joan Green.

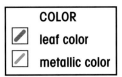

COLOR	
/	leaf color
/	metallic color

Oak Leaf (22 x 37 threads)

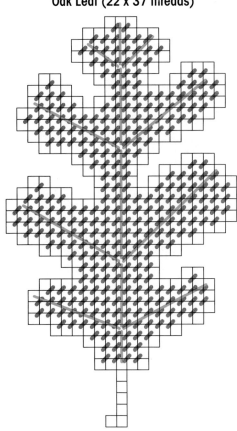

Maple Leaf (24 x 26 threads)

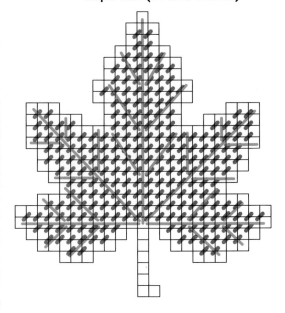

Birch Leaf (18 x 29 threads)

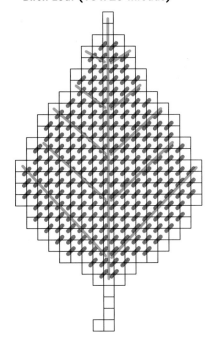

87

Festive Foursome

It'll begin to look a lot like Christmas when this festive foursome catches your eye! The holiday magnets feature some of our favorite symbols of the season — Santa, an angel, and a jolly snowman. They make great ornaments, too.

FESTIVE FOURSOME

Approx. size: 4¹/₂"w x 5"h each

Supplies: Worsted weight yarn (refer to color key), one 10¹/₂" x 13¹/₂" sheet of 7 mesh plastic canvas, #16 tapestry needle, magnetic strip, and craft glue.

Stitches used: French Knot, Overcast Stitch, and Tent Stitch.

Instructions: Follow chart(s) to cut and stitch desired magnet piece(s), working French knots last. Glue magnetic strip to back of magnet.

For Cherub, refer to photo to glue Heart and Leaves to Cherub.

For Santa, refer to photo to glue Mustache to Santa Face.

For Snowman, refer to photo to glue Hat to Snowman.

Designs by Maryanne Moreck.

	COLOR		COLOR
⬜	white	⬜	green
⬜	yellow	⬜	dk green
⬜	gold	⬜	brown
⬜	flesh	⬜	grey
⬜	pink	⬜	black
⬜	red	●	red Fr. knot
⬜	blue	●	black Fr. kno

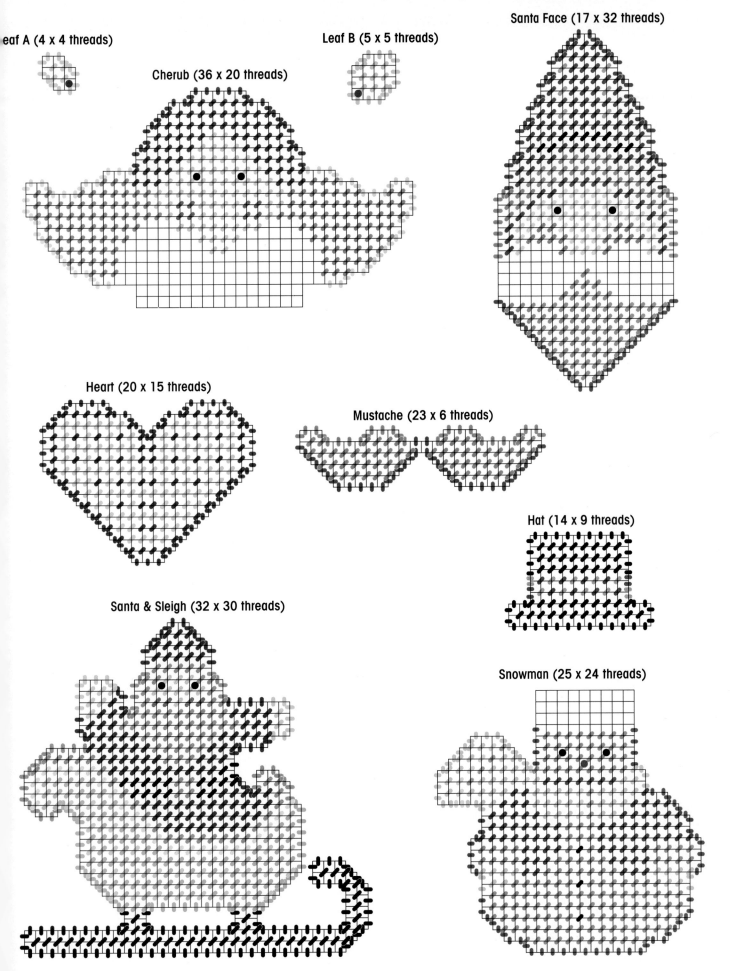

Leaf A (4 x 4 threads)

Cherub (36 x 20 threads)

Leaf B (5 x 5 threads)

Santa Face (17 x 32 threads)

Heart (20 x 15 threads)

Mustache (23 x 6 threads)

Hat (14 x 9 threads)

Santa & Sleigh (32 x 30 threads)

Snowman (25 x 24 threads)

Christmas Memories

This nostalgic collection captures some of our favorite childhood memories of Christmas — ready-to-hug teddies, choo-choo trains, and jingling bells.

CHRISTMAS MEMORIES

Approx. size: 2³/₄"w x 3"h each
Supplies: Worsted weight yarn and Kreinik heavy #32 metallic gold braid (refer to color key), one 10¹/₂" x 13¹/₂" sheet of 7 mesh clear plastic canvas, #16 tapestry needle, magnetic strip, and craft glue.

Stitches used: Backstitch, Cross Stitch, French Knot, Gobelin Stitch, Overcast Stitch, Reversed Tent Stitch, and Tent Stitch.
Instructions: Follow chart to cut and stitch desired magnet, working backstitches and French knots last. Glue magnetic strip to back of magnet.

Designs by Dick Martin.

COLOR		COLOR	
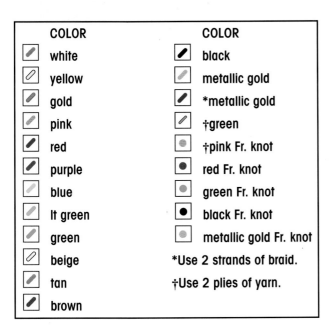 white		black	
yellow		metallic gold	
gold		*metallic gold	
pink		†green	
red		†pink Fr. knot	
purple		red Fr. knot	
blue		green Fr. knot	
lt green		black Fr. knot	
green		metallic gold Fr. knot	
beige			
tan		*Use 2 strands of braid.	
brown		†Use 2 plies of yarn.	

Bell (16 x 16 threads)

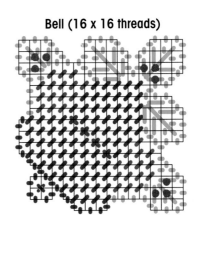

Dog (21 x 21 threads)

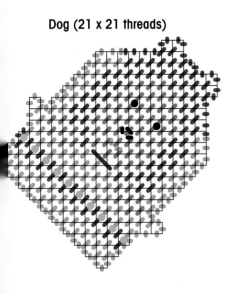

Candle (17 x 16 threads)

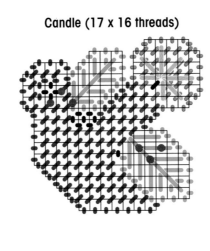

Cat (19 x 21 threads)

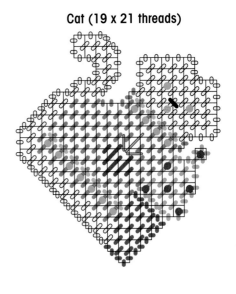

Train (24 x 21 threads)

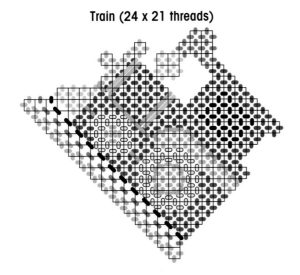

Bear (21 x 21 threads)

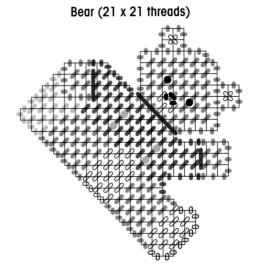

wear green today !

Luck of the Irish

Our curly-bearded leprechaun and simple shamrock will not only give you the luck of the Irish when you display them on your refrigerator, but they'll also make great pins to wear on St. Patrick's Day!

LUCK OF THE IRISH

Approx. size: 1³/₄"w x 2³/₈"h each

Supplies: Sport weight yarn (refer to color key), one 10¹/₂" x 13¹/₂" sheet of 10 mesh plastic canvas, #20 tapestry needle, magnetic strip, and craft glue.

For Leprechaun: Two 6mm moving eyes and one ¹/₄" orange pom-pom.

Stitches used: Backstitch, Cross Stitch, Gobelin Stitch, Overcast Stitch, Tent Stitch, and Turkey Loop.

Instructions: Follow chart(s) to cut and stitch desired magnet piece(s), working backstitches and Turkey loops last. Glue magnetic strip to back of magnet.

For Leprechaun: Refer to photo to glue Brim, Small Shamrock, moving eyes, and pom-pom to Leprechaun.

Leprechaun design by Sandy and Honey for Studio M.

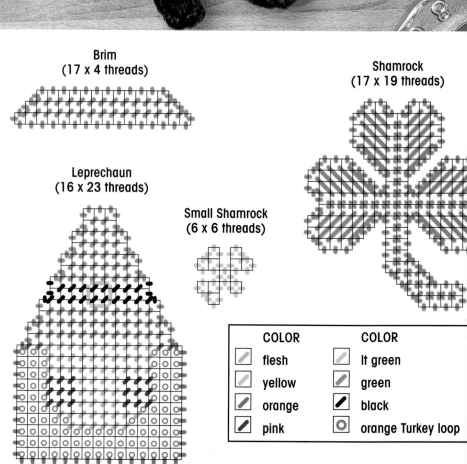

Brim
(17 x 4 threads)

Leprechaun
(16 x 23 threads)

Small Shamrock
(6 x 6 threads)

Shamrock
(17 x 19 threads)

COLOR		COLOR	
/	flesh	/	lt green
/	yellow	/	green
/	orange	/	black
/	pink	⊙	orange Turkey loop

GENERAL INSTRUCTIONS

SELECTING PLASTIC CANVAS

Plastic canvas is a molded material that consists of "threads" and "holes," but the threads aren't actually "threads" since the canvas is not woven. Project instructions often refer to the threads, especially when cutting out plastic canvas pieces. The holes are the spaces between the threads. The Stitch Diagrams, pages 95-96, will refer to holes when explaining where to place your needle to make a stitch.

TYPES OF CANVAS

The main difference between types of plastic canvas is the mesh size. Mesh size refers to the number of holes in one inch of canvas. The projects in this book were stitched using 7 mesh, 10 mesh, or 14 mesh canvas. Seven mesh canvas is the most popular size.

7 mesh = 7 holes per inch
10 mesh = 10 holes per inch
14 mesh = 14 holes per inch

Your project supply list will tell you the size mesh needed for your project. If your project calls for 7 mesh canvas and you use 10 mesh, your finished project will be much smaller than expected.

Most plastic canvas is clear, but colored plastic canvas is also available. Colored canvas is ideal when you don't want to stitch the entire background.

AMOUNT OF CANVAS

The project supply list will tell you how much canvas will be needed to complete a project. As a general rule, it is better to buy too much canvas and have leftovers than to run out of canvas before you finish your project. Most of the individual magnets in this book can be made with scraps or leftover canvas pieces.

SELECTING NEEDLES

TYPES OF NEEDLES

A blunt needle called a tapestry needle is used for stitching on plastic canvas. Tapestry needles are sized by numbers; the higher the number, the smaller the needle. The correct size needle to use depends on the canvas mesh size and the yarn thickness. The needle should be small enough to allow the threaded needle to pass through the canvas holes easily. The eye of the needle should be large enough to allow yarn to be threaded easily. If the eye

is too small, the yarn will wear thin and may break. You will find the recommended needle size listed in the supply section of each project. The chart below will be helpful if you need to select the correct needle for your project.

Mesh	Needle
7	#16 tapestry
10	#20 tapestry
14	#24 tapestry

SELECTING YARN

We have a few hints to help you choose the perfect yarns for your project.

COLORS

Your project will tell you what yarn colors you will need. Brand names and color numbers listed in some color keys are included only as a guide when choosing colors for your project. Choose colors and brands to suit your needs and your taste.

TYPES OF YARN

The types of yarns available are endless, and each grouping of yarn has its own characteristics and uses. The following is a brief description of the yarns used for the magnets in this book.

Worsted Weight Yarn - This yarn may be found in acrylic, wool, wool blends, and a variety of other fiber contents. Worsted weight yarn is the most popular yarn used for 7 mesh plastic canvas because one strand covers the canvas very well. This yarn is inexpensive and comes in a wide range of colors. Worsted weight yarn has four plies that are twisted together to form one strand. When the instructions call for two plies of yarn, you will need to separate a strand of yarn and use only two of the four plies.

Needloft® Plastic Canvas Yarn - This yarn is a 100% nylon worsted weight yarn and is suitable only for 7 mesh canvas. It will not easily separate. When stitching with Needloft and the instructions indicate two plies of yarn, substitute six strands of embroidery floss.

Sport Weight Yarn - Sport weight yarn works nicely for 10 mesh canvas. This yarn has three or four thin plies that are twisted together to form one strand. Like worsted weight yarn, sport weight yarn comes in a variety of fiber contents. The color selection in sport weight yarn is more limited than in

worsted weight yarn. If you can't find sport weight yarn in the color needed, worsted weight yarn may be substituted; simply remove one ply of the yarn and stitch with the remaining three plies.

FLOSS, METALLICS, AND OTHER FIBERS

Embroidery Floss - Embroidery floss is made up of six strands. For smooth coverage when using embroidery floss, separate and realign the strands of floss before threading your needle. Twelve strands of floss may be used for covering 10 mesh canvas. Use six strands to cover 14 mesh canvas. Embroidery floss can also be used to add details on 7 mesh canvas by using six strands of floss.

Metallic Braid or Cord - Metallic braid or cord is available in a variety of sizes and may be used to add finishing details to a project or for general coverage. Using 18" or shorter lengths of metallic braid or cord will make stitching easier and avoid excessive wear.

Metallic Yarn or Ribbon - This flat yarn or ribbon is soft, flexible, and durable. Metallic yarn or ribbon can be used to add decorative details to a project or for general coverage. It is available in different sizes for use with various mesh sizes. Use 18" or shorter lengths of metallic yarn or ribbon for easier stitching and to avoid fraying. Since metallic yarn or ribbon is flat instead of round like other yarns and metallic braids, care must be used to make sure the yarn or ribbon lies flat when stitched on the canvas.

Straw Satin - This rayon, raffia-like material can be used to add a special sheen to your stitching. Using 18" or shorter lengths will make stitching easier and avoid excessive wear.

WORKING WITH PLASTIC CANVAS

Throughout this leaflet, the lines of the canvas will be referred to as threads. To cut plastic canvas pieces accurately, count **threads** (not **holes**) as shown in **Fig. 1**.

Fig. 1

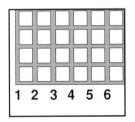

PREPARING AND CUTTING CANVAS

Before cutting out your pieces, note the thread count located above the chart for each piece. The thread count tells you the number of threads in the width and the height of the canvas piece. It can be helpful to follow the thread count to cut out a rectangle the specified size before cutting out your shape. Then, remembering to count **threads**, not **holes,** follow the chart to trim the rectangle into the desired shape.

You may want to use an overhead projector pen to outline the piece on the canvas before cutting it out. Before you begin stitching, be sure to remove all markings with a damp towel. Any markings could rub off on the yarn as you stitch.

If there is room around your chart, it may be helpful to use a ruler and pencil to extend the grid lines of the chart to form a rectangle (see Sample Chart).

Sample Chart

Chicken (18 x 18 threads)

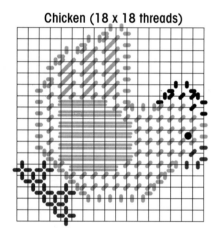

A good pair of household scissors is recommended for cutting plastic canvas. However, a craft knife is helpful when cutting out small areas. When using a craft knife, protect the table below your canvas with a layer of cardboard or a magazine.

When cutting canvas, cut as close to the thread as possible without cutting into the thread. If you don't cut close enough, "nubs" or "pickets" will be left on the edge of your canvas. Make sure to cut all nubs from the canvas before you begin to stitch, because nubs will snag the yarn and are difficult to cover.

When cutting plastic canvas along a diagonal, cut through the center of each intersection **(Fig. 2)**. This will leave enough plastic canvas on both sides of the cut so that both pieces of canvas may be used. Diagonal corners will also snag yarn less and be easier to cover.

Fig. 2

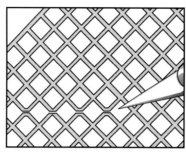

THREADING YOUR NEEDLE

Several brands of yarn-size needle threaders are available at your local craft store. Here are a couple of methods that will make threading your needle easier without a purchased threader.

FOLD METHOD

First, sharply fold the end of yarn over your needle; then remove needle. Keeping the fold sharp, push the needle onto the yarn **(Fig. 3)**.

Fig. 3

THREAD METHOD

Fold a 5" piece of sewing thread in half, forming a loop. Insert loop of thread through the eye of your needle **(Fig. 4)**. Insert yarn through the loop and pull the thread back through your needle, pulling yarn through at the same time.

Fig. 4

READING THE CHART

Whenever possible the drawing on the ch looks like the completed stitch. F example, a tent stitch on the chart is dra diagonally across one intersection threads just like a tent stitch looks wh stitched on your canvas. A symbol will used on the chart when a stitch, such as French knot, cannot be clearly drawn. If y have difficulty determining how a particu stitch should be worked, refer to the list stitches in the project information and Stitch Diagrams on pages 95-96.

READING THE COLOR KEY

A color key is given with each group projects. The key indicates the color us for each stitch on the chart. For examp when white yarn is represented by a g line in the color key, all grey stitches on chart should be stitched using white yarn.

To help you select colors for your projec we have included color numbers Needloft Plastic Canvas Yarn (NL), D Embroidery Floss (DMC), Kreinik Meta Braid and Ribbon (KREINIK), and Dar Straw Satin (DSS) in some of our co keys. Many other different brands available and may be used to stitch yo project.

Additional information may also be inclu in the color key, such as the number strands or plies to use when working particular stitch.

STITCHING THE DESIGN

Securing the First Stitch - Don't knot end of your yarn before you begin stitchi Instead, begin each length of yarn coming up from the wrong side of canvas and leaving a 1" - 2" tail on wrong side. Hold this tail against canvas and work the first few stitches the tail. When secure, clip the tail clos your stitched piece. Clipping the tail clo is important because long tails can beco tangled in future stitches or show throug the right side of the canvas.

Using Even Tension - Keep your stitc tension consistent, with each stitch lying and even on the canvas. Pulling or yank the yarn causes the tension to be too t and you will be able to see through y project. Loose tension is caused by pulling the yarn firmly enou consequently, the yarn will not lie flat on canvas.

...ding Your Stitches - After you've ...mpleted all of the stitches of one color in ...area, end your stitching by running your ...edle under several stitches on the back of ...e stitched piece. To keep the tails of the ...rn from showing through or becoming ...ngled in future stitches, trim the end of the ...rn close to the stitched piece.

...OINING PIECES

...aight Edges - The most common method ...assembling stitched pieces is joining two ...more pieces of canvas along a straight ...ge using overcast stitches. Place one ...ece on top of the other with right or wrong ...es together. Make sure the edges being ...ned are even, then stitch the pieces ...ether through all layers.

...cking - To tack pieces, run your needle ...der the backs of some stitches on one ...ched piece to secure the yarn. Then run ...ur needle through the canvas or under the ...ches on the piece to be tacked in place. ...e idea is to securely attach your pieces ...hout your tacking stitches showing.

...even Edges - Sometimes you'll have to ...n a diagonal edge to a straight edge. The ...les of the two pieces will not line up ...actly. Just keep the pieces even and work ...ercast stitches through holes as many ...es as necessary to completely cover the ...nvas.

...ITCH DIAGRAMS

...nless otherwise indicated, bring ...readed needle up at 1 and all odd ...umbers and down at 2 and all even ...umbers.

...CKSTITCH

...s stitch is worked over completed ...ches to outline or define **(Fig. 5)**. It is ...metimes worked over more than one ...ead. Backstitch may also be used to ...er canvas as shown in **Fig. 6**.

...5

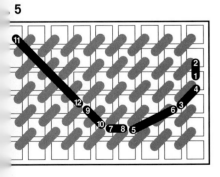

Fig. 6

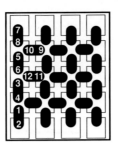

CROSS STITCH

This stitch is composed of two stitches **(Fig. 7)**. The top stitch of each cross must always be made in the same direction. The number of intersections may vary according to the chart.

Fig. 7

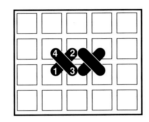

DOUBLE FRENCH KNOT

Bring needle up through hole. Wrap yarn around needle twice and insert needle in same or adjacent hole **(Fig. 8)**. Tighten knot as close to the canvas as possible as you pull the needle and yarn back through canvas.

Fig. 8

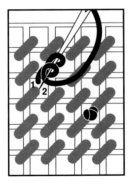

FRENCH KNOT

Bring needle up through hole. Wrap yarn around needle once and insert needle in same or adjacent hole **(Fig. 9)**. Tighten knot as close to the canvas as possible as you pull the needle and yarn back through canvas.

Fig. 9

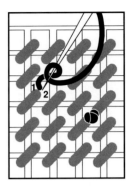

FRINGE STITCH

Fold a length of yarn in half. Thread needle with loose ends of yarn. Bring needle up at 1, leaving a 1" loop on the back of the canvas. Bring needle around the edge of canvas and through loop **(Fig. 10)**. Pull to tighten loop **(Fig. 11)**. Trim fringe to desired length. A dot of glue on back of fringe will help keep stitch in place.

Fig. 10   **Fig. 11**

GOBELIN STITCH

This basic straight stitch is worked over two or more threads or intersections. The number of threads or intersections may vary according to the chart **(Fig. 12)**.

Fig. 12

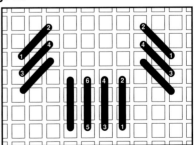

LAZY DAISY STITCH

Bring needle up at 1. Insert needle in the same hole, leaving a loop on top of the canvas. Bring needle up at 2 and through the loop **(Fig. 13)**. To secure loop, insert needle at 2 and gently pull yarn back through canvas until loop lies flat on the canvas.

Fig. 13

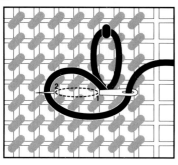

MOSAIC STITCH

This three-stitch pattern forms small squares **(Fig. 14)**.

Fig. 14

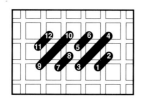

OVERCAST STITCH

This stitch covers the edge of the canvas and joins pieces of canvas **(Fig. 15)**. It may be necessary to go through the same hole more than once to get an even coverage on the edge, especially at the corners.

Fig. 15

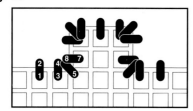

SCOTCH STITCH

This stitch may be worked over three or more threads and forms a square. **Fig. 16** shows the Scotch stitch worked over three threads.

Fig. 16

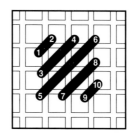

SMYRNA CROSS STITCH

This stitch is worked over two threads as a decorative stitch. Each stitch is worked completely before going on to the next **(Fig. 17)**.

Fig. 17

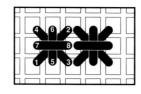

TENT STITCH

This stitch is worked in horizontal or vertical rows over one intersection as shown in **Fig. 18**. Follow **Fig. 19** to work the **reversed tent stitch**.

Fig. 18

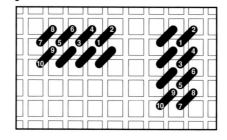

Fig. 19

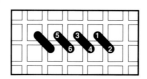

TURKEY LOOP STITCH

This stitch is composed of locked loop Bring needle up through hole and ba down through same hole, forming a lo on top of the canvas. A locking stitch then made across the thread directly bel or to either side of loop as shown in **Fig. 2**

Fig. 20

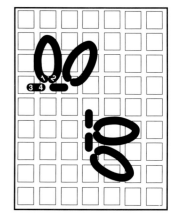

UPRIGHT CROSS STITCH

This stitch is worked over two threads shown in **Fig. 21**. The top stitch of ea cross must always be made in the sa direction.

Fig. 21

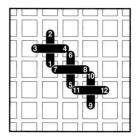

WASHING INSTRUCTIONS

If you used washable yarn for all of y stitches, you may hand wash plas canvas projects in warm water with a r soap. Do not rub or scrub stitches; this cause the yarn to fuzz. Do not dry-clear put your stitched pieces in a clothes dr Allow pieces to air dry and trim any f with a small pair of sharp scissors o sweater shaver.

Some photography models made by J Akins, Toni Bowden, Gary Hutcheson, Connie McGaughey.

#1807 $15.9

0 28906 01807 3

ISBN 1-57486-096-8